REAL INSIGHTS

BY JOHN GRAFF

ISBN: 979-8-9852750-0-1 (paperback)

First Edition published by Ellimat Books 2021

Please contact the author at:

john@ashbygraff.com

For Matthew, Elliott, and Cuthbert—my boys.

Contents

Introduction

As you prepare to launch your real estate career, you understandably have high hopes for the future. You may know of real estate agents in your area who have a great work-life balance and who maintain an enviable lifestyle. In fact, those successful real estate agents may have inspired you to start your career in this industry.

Depending on which state you are based out of, you may be eyeing an average income of between $40,000 to $65,000. Of course, successful real estate agents can achieve an income that far surpasses the six-figure threshold. This income, combined with the ability to set your own work hours, can seem amazing to someone who is coming off a 9-to-5 grind. That is understandably where your focus is centered. That is what may have pushed you to persevere through your real estate courses.

However, dreaming will not get you where you want to be. The difference between a dream and a goal is a plan. What is your plan after you get licensed?

No real estate agent starts out expecting to fail, but the unfortunate reality is that 87 percent of real estate agents will move on to new career opportunities within their first five years on the job.

There is not a single reason why many new real estate agents throw in the towel, although most of them likely stem from that gray area between dreams and goals. Everything from rapidly changing market conditions to unrealistic expectations about the job and dozens of other reasons could be to blame. Do you have a plan to get through these obstacles, or will you simply continue dreaming about turning over big commission checks?

After you spend months studying to pass the licensing exam and lining up a great broker to work with, you may think that you are positioned for success. But remember, your license is a basic requirement that every new real estate agent must have—it is not a golden ticket. The majority of people who cover the basics by getting licensed will fail in this line of work.

What can you do to set yourself apart from other agents and be part of that 13 percent of real estate agents who have a long and successful career?

A Long, Winding Road Ahead

The reality is that the real estate industry is in a constant state of flux. In fact, it has historically had a fairly reliable cycle with both recessionary dips and profitable peaks. The industry is also intricately linked to a variety of other factors. These include the Fed's monetary policy, the mortgage industry, the cost of building supplies, the labor market, and more. It is simply not reasonable to expect your career to be insulated from the ups and downs related to real estate cycles.

Of course, there are a variety of other challenges that you must contend with while navigating through the cyclical ups and downs. For example, you must be able to successfully find potential new clients who are ready to buy or sell soon. Then, you must win over those leads by converting them into clients. This is often easier said than done. After all, other real estate agents will be competing for their business as well.

Once you have sold yourself successfully to a client, you must rely on your knowledge of the local real estate market, harness your negotiation skills, and navigate through a series of pitfalls on each transaction you complete. Rest assured that no two transactions will be the same, and each one will present you with learning opportunities and a few headaches.

There are other challenges to contend with on a more personal level. For example, many people who have been salaried employees underestimate how challenging it can be to stay motivated to put in full-time hours when they do not have regular oversight from a manager. Others may grow frustrated with the fact that they are working so hard now and may not have any financial gains to show for it for a few months down the road. Then there are challenges related to time management, organization, communication, work-life balance, technological expertise, and more.

Education Is the Key to Success

Do you feel discouraged? Before you start to second-guess your new career path, take a deep breath. You are not confronting all of these challenges at once.

You are also not recreating the wheel. While each day as a real estate agent will be filled with experiences that are new to you, they are not necessarily new to the many other real estate agents who came before you. The reality is that you do not have to personally endure all of the stressors associated with launching a new real estate career. Instead, you can focus on education. The more you can learn now, the smoother your path ahead may be.

The most successful real estate agents do not have a know-it-all mentality; they embrace the fact that they still have a lot to learn despite their many years in the business. They also accept the fact that the industry is constantly changing, technologies are evolving, and relationships are growing.

Real estate is not a career where you will ultimately have all of the answers at all times. Instead, it is a career where you will always have the opportunity to grow by expanding your knowledge base and fine-tuning your skills. Your success as a real estate agent is directly linked to education. While you could wait for learning opportunities to hit you in the face, a better idea is to be proactive and seek educational opportunities.

The good news is that you do not have to learn all of the lessons through hard knocks. Instead, you can rely on this guide to navigate some of the more common challenges that new real estate agents face. Each chapter in this guide is filled with insights covering everything from marketing and developing relationships with clients to refining your pricing strategies and more.

By learning more about the challenges that lie in front of you in the months and years to come, you can better prepare yourself for navigating around obstacles that you will inevitably be faced with. After all, you do not necessarily need to endure stress and lose sleep in order to learn the ropes as a real estate agent.

Your Journey Starts Here

As you start your career in real estate, you can and should celebrate the fact that you have aced your courses and passed the licensing exam. In fact, you should celebrate each accomplishment regardless of how seemingly small it is.

You may be inclined to use your commission checks as a yardstick to gauge success. While this is one metric that you can use, understand that there are others. Real estate is a relationship business. Your ability to establish and cultivate relationships is key to your success. With this in mind, another metric to gauge success on is the number of leads you convert into customers. You can also use your referral stats, the deviation between list and sales prices, and a variety of other factors to gauge success in your new career.

At the same time, you should not use "failure" as a label. Your broad professional goals will likely not deviate. Those goals include converting leads, winning clients, and closing deals. While these are desired outcomes, an alternative outcome is not necessarily a failure. For example, you may have not earned business from the last client you met with, but did you learn how to overcome a new sales objection or how to improve your pricing strategy in a competitive market analysis?

It was not a failure if you learned something from it. Learning opportunities give you the chance to become a better real estate agent.

With this in mind, you can see that passing your licensing exam does not open the door to a leisurely lifestyle and tons of high-dollar commission checks. It is not a threshold where learning stops and earning starts. Instead, it can be viewed as the first step in a long journey. That journey continues as you use the resources in this guide to improve your knowledge base and to grow as a real estate agent.

1

How to Get Your Real Estate License

If you are already licensed, you can skip ahead to Chapter 2, but if you have yet to receive your real estate license, this chapter is definitely for you. Each state regulates its own licensing processes with rules that differ from state to state. Above all, there are a few general requirements that remain consistent:

- You must be over 18 years of age to practice as a real estate agent.
- You must hold a valid United States residency.
- You must complete the required pre-licensed education.
- You must pass your state's real estate license exam.

The specifics tend to vary from one state to the next, but generally, there are seven steps to becoming a licensed real estate agent.

Step 1: Meet Your State's Licensing Requirements

Visit your state's real estate commission website. This official website will list all pre-licensing requirements. In most states, 60-90 hours of college-level education in real estate basics is required to qualify for a license. You can find these courses through a simple internet search, and there are options for you to take the classes in person, live online, or on demand. Keep in mind that the licensing school you choose to study with must be accredited and acknowledged by your state.

Step 2: Complete a Pre-Licensing Course

While the cost of pre-licensing courses differs, bear in mind that becoming a real estate agent requires both time and investment—just like any other business venture.

Some pre-licensing courses are set over a number of weeks, while others allow you to finish in your own time and move at your own pace. It really just depends on which course provider you choose and the type of class you select. You'll need to choose the best course to fit your lifestyle and the amount of study you can manage in a designated timeframe. You can expect to pay between $200-$1,000 for your courses, depending on your state and the school you choose to study with.

Step 3: Submit Your Application for the Real Estate Exam

You must be sure to follow the application process carefully. This way, you'll be able to sit for your real estate exam soon after you've completed your studies. The process is specific to your state and the fees will vary, but most states will require fingerprints and a background check before scheduling an exam date. These details can take several weeks to process, so make sure this part of your application is completed as early as possible.

Step 4: Sit for Your Real Estate Exam and Pass!

It's important to know that not everyone passes the real estate exam the first time, and that's okay. That's why preparation and adequate study is so important.

It's recommended that you enroll in the exam preparation class, especially if it's been a good few years since you last studied or took an exam. These classes allow you to take practice exams and work on your strengths, weaknesses, and build up your comprehension of certain subjects. By putting in a little bit of additional work, you can be assured of passing the first time and be well on your way to kick-starting your career.

Tips to Pass Your Real Estate Exam:

- Stop reading stories on the internet where people talk about failing one or more times. This does nothing for your mind and confidence. Quite honestly, it's a waste of time.
- Use a few resources. Too many resources will overwhelm you and prevent you from focusing. We strongly recommend Real Estate Express for real estate exam prep.
- Obtain an outline of the test content. This document will tell you what you will be tested on and how many questions from each section will be on the test. Use the outline (from your state) as an additional study aide.
- Pay attention in class. Your teacher will share stories and examples that will help you remember important information.
- Read the books and create an outline. By writing the outline, you will focus on key information and it will help you retain the information for test day.
- Complete all practice questions, quizzes, and tests (don't write in the book) more than once. If you have access to an online question bank, use it! The more questions you do, the stronger you will become.

Bonus Tips (For When You Have to Guess)

Regardless of how thoroughly you prepare, there will be some questions on the Real Estate Exam that you don't know the answer to; some, you won't be able to make an educated guess about. Follow these rules to increase your odds of guessing correctly:

- If two of the test answer options are opposites, choose one of those two.
- If two of the four test answers are almost identical, choose the longer one.
- Pay attention to words like "always" and "never." Few things in life are "always" or "never." Be suspicious of these answers.
- The word "except" can turn an exam question around. When you see this word in either the question or one or more of the answers, make a mental note of it.
- General terms such as "most," "some," and "usually" are more likely to be found in a correct answer.
- Distrust exaggerated or complex exam answers.
- If you've never heard of it before, don't select it.
- Answer every question, even if you're guessing. Unanswered questions are marked wrong. There is no penalty for guessing.

Step 5: Secure a Real Estate Brokerage

Once you've passed your real estate exam, this doesn't mean you're free to begin practicing independently. You need to be affiliated and work under a licensed real estate broker.

Try and find a real estate broker as early as possible in your licensing process. Once you have completed your studies and passed your exam, you and your broker can complete final paperwork and submit it to the state. After you have been accepted by the state, your license will be issued and you'll be free to practice under the sponsorship of your new broker. More details about landing at a real estate brokerage can be found in Chapter 4.

Step 6: Join the NAR

Another important step once you've been granted your real estate license is to join the National Association of Realtors (NAR). While it's not legally necessary, it's a requirement in order to do business under the designation of REALTOR®. This also helps when looking to participate in Multiple Listing Services, or MLS. Without access to MLS, your earning potential could be severely limited, so it's definitely worth joining the NAR. You gain membership in the National Association of Realtors by joining a local association. A quick internet search of your city plus "association of realtors" should give you some local association options. Once you join the local association, you will automatically become a member of your state association of realtors as well as the National Association of Realtors.

Step 7: Remember the Importance of License Renewal

Securing your real estate license is a lot of work and expense—don't let it all go to waste because you neglected your license renewal! Make sure to double-check your state's licensing requirements and how often a real estate license should be renewed. This is generally every two to four years. You'll also need to complete a number of hours of additional course study in order to be eligible for renewal. This ranges from 22-90 hours every two years. These courses are relevant to ensure real estate agents are kept up to date on ever-changing state markets and regulations. Try and take care of your continuing education requirements as soon as possible and don't push it off. I've seen too many agents lose access to their real estate license just because they waited too long to submit the renewal and their license lapsed. It's just not worth the added stress and hassle.

2

Why New Agents Fail

The data on first-year real estate agents is brutally clear. After spending time, money, and energy getting licensed and finding a broker to work under, most real estate agents quit before their first anniversary. While this unfortunate statistic seemingly indicates that the majority of new agents are making the same errors, the reality is that there are many pitfalls and challenges that new agents face. Any one of these challenges may be enough to cause an inexperienced real estate agent to throw in the towel, and the unfortunate reality is that real estate agents often struggle with multiple challenges as they learn the ropes.

While starting a new career as a real estate agent can be both demanding and stressful, you may be able to save yourself some grief through improved knowledge and proper planning. When you know what challenges lie ahead, you can take steps either to navigate around them or to wade confidently through them. What are the top issues that new real estate agents run into during their first year on the job?

Lack of a Business Plan

Commonly, real estate agents initially believe that their brokerage firm will provide them with a solid foundation to launch off of. This may include everything from guidance on marketing to lead generation and more. The actual level of support that a broker provides varies dramatically, but most new real estate agents are dismayed to learn that their expectations are not met in this area.

As is the case when you launch any new business venture, you need to have a clear, well-researched plan of action, and you need to be ready to fully execute all aspects of that plan. Before your first day on the job, you need to identify who your target audience is and what territory you want to cover. Think about how you will market to those individuals and what your message will be. Some of the many other important areas to plan ahead for are your marketing budget, prospecting opportunities, lead nurturing, and relationship building.

Unrealistic Expectations

If you believe that a professional career as a real estate agent will lead you to loads of easy money, rest assured that you are not the only person to have this assumption—an assumption that turns out to be not all that true. You may find that showing homes to clients is as fun and as enjoyable as the

TV shows make it seem to be. However, cold-calling, following up on mediocre leads, preparing comparative market analysis reports, and sifting through data require hard work, and these critical aspects of the job are often overlooked by aspiring real estate agents.

The reality is that the average income for a real estate agent is approximately $40,000. While some real estate agents earn well above six figures, others struggle to make ends meet. The idea that real estate equates to fast, easy money is often quickly dashed. This disillusion often leads to frustration and detracts from motivation. Establishing realistic goals related to your income and to the amount of effort the job requires from day one is important.

Inadequate Financial Support

There are two primary reasons why new real estate agents need to have adequate financial support. One of these reasons is because it may be months before you close your first deal. These are months when you will be putting in hours of daily effort and you will not see a penny in return. How will you pay your bills during these months? You must have a plan in place so that you can avoid financial stress and concentrate on your career.

The other reason for having a healthy nest egg to draw from is that you will need to invest in marketing. Whether you are mailing out postcards to a community, handing out brochures at an open house, or fine-tuning your website with new features, you need to have a healthy marketing budget available. Nurturing this aspect of your business upfront will lay a solid foundation that you can build upon.

Not Putting in Full-Time Effort

Were you attracted to a career in real estate because of its flexible work hours and a shorter workweek? Real estate agents are generally on call to field inquiries and to serve clients most or all days of the week. More than that, clients expect to be able to reach a real estate agent far beyond traditional business hours. The reality is that you will put in long hours as a real estate agent.

When you are starting out, you may not have clients to serve yet. Your inclination may be that you can start later in the day and stop working in the middle of the afternoon. After all, you may have made a few calls, and your phone is not ringing. However, you must set the wheels of your business in motion through many hours spent working hard. Even after you land a few clients, you must keep pedaling so that you do not lose the traction that you have worked hard to establish.

Lack of Marketing Knowledge

If you think that you know everything you need to know about marketing, you may want to reconsider that assumption. Professional marketers go to school for years to learn their trade, and they continue to learn on the job to keep up with the changing landscape and new technologies. It is not enough to rely on the single page of digital real estate that your broker provides to you or to make a few social media posts from time to time as your sole marketing efforts.

Instead, you must identify who your target audience is and refine your message to your audience so that it is increasingly relevant and effective. At the same time, you must find a solid way to get in front of those individuals regularly so that you are the real estate agent they turn to when they are ready to buy or sell. Developing your brand and building relationships are rooted in marketing as well.

Poor Prospecting Skills

Few new real estate agents revel in the idea of making cold calls and hunting down leads. For some people, this is rather humiliating. For others, it is a frustratingly slow process that seemingly has little benefit. Many new agents assume that they will not need to prospect and that their broker will hand them all of the leads that they need to start securing clients and closing deals.

However, prospecting is an important part of the real estate business. It generates leads, and leads drive sales. Without prospecting, you are essentially waiting for your phone to ring rather than making things happen yourself. Working with a broker that offers opportunities to answer the phone and to reach out to online leads is important, but you also need to be eager to make the first contact.

Not Learning from Mistakes

You can see that new real estate agents can and do make many mistakes. Mistakes can eat away at your confidence and may cause you to have second thoughts about your ability to succeed as a real estate agent. While you could let mistakes wear you down, you could look at them in another way. Mistakes are learning opportunities. You learned what not to do, so now you have a better idea of what to do.

Successful real estate agents did not make confident steps at every turn. They ran into the same mistakes that other real estate agents did. The main difference between them and the agents who gave up is that they learned and persevered through challenges. You may be able to sidestep many common challenges that first-year real estate agents make by simply studying their efforts. After all, you do not need to recreate the wheel. However, you will still make a few mistakes, and you must have the tenacity to learn your lessons and to keep moving forward.

If the real estate business were as easy and as lucrative as most new agents assume that it will be, there would be many more real estate agents in the world. The fact that so many first-year real estate agents throw in the towel is a sure sign that this is a challenging business with a steep learning curve. Now that you have a better idea about what to expect from your new career as a real estate agent, you can take steps now to better prepare yourself for the road in front of you.

3

The Traits Shared by Successful Agents

There are certain traits that the most successful real estate agents have. When you gather up all the top performers and really look at what they are doing that is working and then you distill that data and compare it amongst the bunch, you find a few core skills that set the stage for much of their success.

Successful Agents Respond FAST

So we know that successful agents treat real estate like a career. But what are some other ways that they are united in their success? Successful agents stand out among the competition by responding fast. We live in an age of instant gratification, from Amazon Prime, where you can have items delivered next day or even the same day, to Netflix, where you can watch an entire season of a television show in one evening, to the new trend of iBuyers that threaten to shake up the industry (more on that later).

Customers nowadays want things fast. So when a potential client calls you and they reach your voice-mail, they may very well just hang up and call the next agent on their list. If you are able to answer the phone right away or reply to emails in minutes instead of hours, you are going to impress lots of customers and clients. And when their friends complain to them about their real estate agent who hasn't responded to the email they sent last night, your client can rave about how amazingly fast and responsive their agent is.

Do you think there is a chance that your client's friend may want to know your contact information after that?

Successful Agents Keep in Touch

The very best agents are ones who are always staying in touch with their clients; that includes ones who have closed transactions with them, as well as clients that they have or are currently working with but haven't yet closed a deal with. Good agents genuinely care about their clients and are typically good with people. When these agents touch base with their clients, they are often not discussing real estate—they're staying in touch about kids and pets, work, birthdays and anniversaries, and current events.

You should definitely sprinkle in information related to real estate, but it should be organic. Clients will naturally ask you, "How is the market doing?" or "My neighbor said they were thinking about selling.

How much do you think their house is worth?" This is your opportunity to discuss real estate topics. You can also bring up real estate if there is something really relevant and newsworthy that you feel your clients should really know about. The point is, real estate is a relationship business, so you want to develop meaningful relationships with your customers and your clients. That is how you are going to get repeat business and new business via referrals from and to their friends and family.

Successful Agents Stay in the Know

Top agents know what's happening in the industry. They stay educated and pay attention to market trends. There are so many resources online and otherwise for real estate agents: Inman, RISMedia, REALTrends, and your state or local *REALTOR* magazine. The best agents are well read and know what's happening in the industry before everyone else; they have their pulse on things by staying curious and constantly learning.

Continuing education isn't just something you need to do every few years to renew your real estate license. You can use it to pursue professional designations and certifications that will help you stand out from your competition. That's in addition to the serious knowledge you'll be gaining from focusing on your education. Some designations and certifications can be completed totally online, so you can sign up and complete the course all from the comfort of your home.

Successful agents also attend industry events. Many of the same publishers mentioned earlier also host annual conferences and other gatherings for networking and learning. Your local and state realtor associations also put on events and other training or educational sessions that can either be accessed in person or online. You could also look into coaching events such as those run by Tom Ferry and Buffini. There are also numerous multicultural organizations in the real estate industry, like the National Association of Hispanic Real Estate Professionals (NAHREP), the Asian American Real Estate Association (AAREA), the National Association of Real Estate Brokers (NAREB), and groups serving the needs of the LGBTQ community. Even if you are not a member of any of these communities, these groups welcome all allies as members of their respective organizations.

Successful Agents Are Goal Oriented

The importance of setting goals and meeting goals cannot be overstated. All successful people are good at setting and realizing goals. In the real estate industry, you can have different types of goals depending on what specific field you are working in, but if you're in residential sales, one goal you should track is "contacts made."

Types of Goals to Track

Contacts Made

Contacts made is the number of potential clients you have contacted in a certain amount of time.

Tracking the number of contacts you make is important because eventually you will learn your conversion rate or the number of contacts that then turn into appointments. If you make 100 contacts in a week, not all 100 of them are going to agree to make an appointment to meet with you. It is not reasonable to expect that. It is more reasonable to expect one or two of those 100 contacts to agree to make an appointment with you. Whatever goal you set, make sure it is reasonable and attainable. At the same time you don't want to make it too easy. As you are just getting started, it will be a bit of a guessing game, but as a rule I like to increase my goals between 0 and 10 percent depending on my forecast for the year ahead.

Appointments Set

As mentioned, you will also want to track appointments set. In these appointments that you have with customers, your ultimate goal is to get an agreement signed.

Listing or Buyer Representation Agreements Signed

You are either hoping to have a home seller sign a listing agreement with you or have a home buyer sign a buyer representation agreement with you. Once the customer signs a contract to be represented by you, they become a client.

Homes under Contract

It will be essential to track the number of homes that you put under contract—that is to say, homes that are currently pending sale where you represent either one or both sides of the transaction. It's important to keep in mind that the average timeframe to sell a home once it's under contract can vary depending on certain conditions and where you are located, but on average it's safe to assume it takes between 30 and 60 days to close a home purchase transaction. Unfortunately, just having a contract does not mean it will successfully make it all the way to closing. Deals fall out of escrow all the time for a variety of reasons. So keep in mind that not every home you get under contract will wind up selling in that particular contract.

Homes Sold

Because not every home under contract sells, agents also track the number of homes sold in a set amount of time. By tracking all of these numbers and comparing them over time, and against each other, you will eventually be able to set realistic—but aggressive—goals that will continue to push you toward excellence in the field.

Successful Agents Follow Routines

Are you good at following routines? Well, some of the most successful real estate agents are absolute pros at routine setting and following. By no means does this mean that you have to wake up at 4 a.m.

and go for a three-hour jog before hopping on the phone for six hours straight before you can eat lunch. You can if you want, but often that mentality just ends in burnout.

That said, whatever routine you set, just make sure it is one that is realistic for you to follow and that you will have the discipline to actually follow it. This does not mean you have to do the same thing every single day only to become bogged down by boredom. But it does mean that you have systems in place to replicate known processes that are essential to your success. And these can be little things too. Things as minor as waking up at the same time every day, eating breakfast, exercising, and devoting time to reading are all examples of routines that some of the most successful people share.

Successful Agents Follow Their Hearts

An ancient Greek expression often (though falsely) attributed to Socrates says, "nosce te ipsum" or "know thyself"—a maxim for the ages, and for good reason. Knowing yourself, knowing what you excel at and regularly achieve—while also knowing your limitations and liabilities—is a key part of the recipe for successful real estate agents.

Find what you are good at and keep doing it as much as you can. Pass off to others the work that you are not so good at. This is harder when you are just getting started, of course, but the easiest and earliest example of this that you will see is working with a transaction coordinator. A transaction coordinator, or TC, as they are commonly referred to in the industry, is someone who assists licensed real estate agents with transactional documents and other aspects of a transaction, like staying on timelines, keeping track of parties to the transaction (like title officer, buyers, and sellers), as well as helping to make sure documents are filled out properly and completely. Real estate brokerages will often offer TC services to agents for a small fee, usually between $300 and $600. You can also find transaction coordinators available for hire online.

Quick Tip: While it might be tempting to use a transaction coordinator for your first transaction, I would strongly advise against it. At the very least, you should view the transaction coordinator on your first transaction as a backup or a second set of eyes looking over your documents. As the real estate agent, or the expert, you really do need to have an understanding of everything that is involved in the process from start to finish. And you really should have a thorough knowledge and understanding of the most commonly used real estate contracts in your area. By succumbing to the temptation to just pass all this work off to your transaction coordinator, you will likely miss out on essential lessons and skills that you should have. You need to do this work yourself in the beginning so you see what goes into it. This will make you a better real estate expert for your clients.

But even beyond the day-to-day tasks that you will either be doing or be passing off to others to do on your behalf, you will need to be able to follow your heart and your brain to lead you to where you want to be.

If you have been working with buyers for the past eleven months and all you can think about is how much you enjoyed working with sellers on the two listings you had just last year, then maybe that is a sign that you should be spending more of your time trying to get listings instead of working with buyer clients. Whenever possible, focus your energy and attention on the things that you do well and that bring you joy; this is a key to success.

Listen to your heart and follow it.

The Two Most Vital Lessons All Agents Learn Their First Year in Business

As a new real estate agent, you are understandably eager to jump head first into the water with your first client. This could lead you to make hasty decisions when the first potential lead comes along—or even to solicit friends and family members without weighing the pros and cons first. While your passion for your new career can take you far, your eagerness could lead you to experience some hard knocks unnecessarily.

The reality is that many real estate agents have learned hard lessons related to client selection. Fortunately, these are not lessons that you have to experience first-hand. By learning from others who have stood in your shoes, you can develop valuable insight about client selection. While you will undoubtedly develop your own vetting process when working with new clients, these are the two lessons that you can use to get your career off on a solid footing.

Lesson 1: Your Family and Friends Do Not Owe You Business

In some cases, brokers advise new real estate agents to tap into their personal network of family members, friends, and acquaintances to find a few clients. After all, you may know people who plan to buy or sell real estate soon. You already have great relationships with these people, so it makes sense to leverage those relationships for your financial gain. At the same time, you know that you can give them the personal attention they deserve throughout their transaction.

While representing family and friends can initially seem like a win-win situation, many new real estate agents are dismayed to find out that their close contacts have other plans in mind. It can seem insulting at first glance that your contacts would rather work with a complete stranger than with you. However, there are several legitimate reasons why many people prefer to buy and sell real estate without relying on a friend or a family member for representation.

Separating Business and Personal Lives

While you may be agreeable to joining your business and personal lives together, this may not be the same for some of your close contacts. Perhaps they have been burned in the past or have heard nightmarish stories from their other acquaintances about comparable situations. In many cases, when a person does not want someone close to them to represent them in a deal, they do not want to risk ruining a great relationship by mixing business and pleasure. This does not mean that they lack confidence in your abilities; it means that they value your relationship.

Keeping Finances Private

As a real estate agent, you may be privy to many personal details about a client. Over the course of a transaction, you may see documents showing the loan amount that they are prequalified for and the associated interest rate. You likely will see what their new mortgage payment may be. These factors may reveal things about their finances that they prefer to keep private, such as a low credit score or their personal income. You can be friends with someone for decades and never learn this information, so it makes sense that they may not want you to know this private information about them right now.

Lacking Experience or Knowledge

A real estate transaction has far-reaching ramifications on a person's life. After all, both personal finances and housing are serious matters that are directly impacted by the purchase or sale of a home. As a new real estate agent, your lack of professional experience can give your friends and family members a legitimate reason to have concerns. Perhaps your experience has not come into question, but your lack of negotiation skills in a hot market, your lack of knowledge about a niche area of real estate, or other matters may be concerns.

Just as your family and friends may have concerns about hiring you as their real estate agent, there may be reasons why you should have second thoughts about representing them. What are some of the cons that you should be aware of before you work for someone you have a pre-existing relationship with?

Unrealistic Expectations and Standards

Most real estate transactions have at least a few blips, and many have major hurdles that must be overcome in order to reach the desired endpoint. Regardless of whether you are representing friends, family, or new acquaintances, there is a possibility that they may not have realistic expectations. Perhaps they expect the entire transaction to go smoothly, to win a heated bidding war, or even for you to be available at all hours of the day and night. It can be more difficult to establish realistic expectations and to set professional limits with people who are close to you.

When Deals Go Bad

Even with your best effort, there are deals that will unfortunately not go as well as planned. What happens then? Your clients may lose money, be temporarily homeless while they search for another home, and more. You understandably want the best outcome for all of your clients, but do you really want to deal with the potential ramifications of a deal gone bad? Keep in mind that this could taint their view of you for years to come.

Professional Incompatibility

You may get along perfectly well with someone as neighbors, friends, or family members, but that does not necessarily mean you should do business with them. Many people find that they are not professionally compatible with people who they otherwise get along well with. If this is the case, your relationship may become strained and awkward until after closing.

The Potential Impact on a Great Relationship

Real estate transactions are stressful. In addition to your need to get paid for all of your work by closing the transaction, your clients have their own significant motivators. Even the strongest friendships or familial relationships can get stressed when matters like money and housing are at stake. When you accept a friend or a family member as a client, there is always a possibility of developing bad blood. Is the risk of possibly ruining a relationship worth a possible commission?

The Matter of Compensation

One of the reasons why some of your friends and family members may consider hiring you as their real estate agent is to save money. Sellers may be eager to cut your commission down to a point or two, or they may even ask you to work on their deal for several long weeks or months without getting paid at all. On the other hand, buyers may know that you are getting a sizable commission check, and they may ask you to give them a cut of it. While some real estate agents are willing to do this, the thought of working just as hard or even harder for someone you know and earning less money for your effort can be disheartening.

Resentment

You do not need to be a real estate agent for very long to know that this is hard work. However, there is a misconception that representing clients is easy work and that real estate agents lead cushy lives. While representing a friend or a family member could potentially give them an inside look into the hard work that your job demands, it could also breed resentment if they fail to see your efforts through the right lens.

While these are all legitimate concerns, they may not be relevant in all situations. After all, many people have successfully represented their friends and family members in transactions. As you move forward, understand that their decision not to ask for your assistance should not be taken personally. In fact, such a decision could be in both of your best interests. Your friends and family members will likely carefully weigh the pros and cons on their end, and you should do the same. If both parties feel that your representation is best for them, you can confidently move forward. If one or both parties have legitimate concerns, however, understand that those concerns are valid.

Lesson 2: You Will Encounter Shady Clients When You Are Starting Out

It is clear why you should be cautious about working for friends or family members, but this does not mean that you should view everyone else in your community as a potential client. Experienced real estate agents know precisely how to screen new leads so that they only concentrate their time and energy on those with the greatest potential.

As a new real estate agent, you may not know how to properly vet your clients. At the same time, you may think that you should work with anyone who is willing so that you can generate revenue. Regardless of how challenging the client is, he or she is still someone you can learn from and use as a reference. While this is true, new real estate agents' willingness to accept just about anyone as a new client may be one of the reasons why they are magnets for shady clients.

Many real estate agents have suffered hard knocks because of their poor client selection. The good news is that you can gain valuable knowledge about being selective without having to endure the stress that your predecessors went through.

Understanding Shady Clients

The first step in selecting great clients involves identifying shady people. By definition, a shady person is someone who lies, sneaks around, or stabs someone in the back. When you initially communicate with a lead, it will likely be over the phone or via email. Can you tell from the initial communication if a person is shady? If you receive a long, rambling email message where the sender contradicts himself or herself several times, this could be a red flag. Most initial communications, however, are short inquiries. Other efforts to identify shady clients are needed.

Some people may appear to be shady, but they may actually be indecisive or uncertain. For example, someone may backtrack on what they initially told you they wanted in a house because they spent more time reflecting on it. On the other hand, someone may tell you that they are relocating from out of town when they actually live on the other side of town with their parents. While the latter situation may seem like a white lie, it actually can signify that the person cannot be trusted. After all, if they will lie about something that is seemingly innocent, would they lie about something that could ultimately impact the deal?

The Impact of Poor Clients on Your Career

Shady clients can zap you of time and energy. This is time and energy that you could have spent working for other clients. At the same time, these clients can cause headaches, unnecessary delays, and even unsurpassable obstacles that ultimately kill the deal. When you work for a client who is not on the up-and-up, there is a solid chance that you may spin your wheels for weeks on end and never get paid for your efforts.

There are other consequences to consider as well. For example, there is a strong likelihood that the transaction will end on a sour note. A shady person may be of questionable character, so he or she could post negative reviews, spread poor word-of-mouth information, or even file a false report about you. These are issues that could impact your future livelihood for years to come in some cases

On the other hand, if you take time to properly vet your clients upfront, you may be more likely to close the deal and get paid what your time and energy are worth. You may also generate great referrals and a prime review, and these can help you to build your career.

How to Screen Your Clients

What can you do to weed out the duds so that you can focus your attention on career-building clients? One important step is to take time getting to know each new lead. This can help you provide better service throughout the transaction as well, so it serves a dual purpose. Rather than have a single, extended conversation, break it up into a few different sessions. Ensure that the person is easy to get in touch with and does not contradict himself or herself about things that should be hard facts. Ask getting-to-know-you questions that may reveal if the person is concealing or lying about something.

Not all professional relationships with new leads work out, but a lead who has already spent time working with one agent should put up a red flag. If a deal fell through, ask what happened. This information can help you to determine if you need to take a better approach to serve the client or if there is an ongoing issue that he or she is trying to cover up. Is the client badmouthing the former real estate agent? Often, a small amount of digging will uncover the truth.

Also, pay attention to follow-through. Does the lead respond promptly to texts and phone calls? Is he or she easy to get in touch with? Is communication clear and friendly? Does the client cancel meetings or show up late? If you have trouble with the lead at this stage in the transaction, you can likely expect that experience to continue.

You understandably want to jump at the chance to work with any clients who show interest in the early stage of your career, but you can see that doing so can have long-term, damaging effects. Remember that there are many other fish in the sea. If you have legitimate reasons to be concerned about working with a potential client, this could be a sign that it is best to move on.

4

How to Find the Right Brokerage to Work For

It is never too early to start searching for a broker to work under, and if you already joined a brokerage, you should take time to determine if you have partnered with a broker who will support you on your path toward a successful career. Some new real estate agents are intimidated about interviewing brokers, but this effort can ultimately yield exceptional returns over the long run. Keep in mind that brokers make money off their relationships with real estate agents. This means that they are equally interested in finding great real estate agents to sponsor.

The Critical Need for a Licensed Broker

Many people use the terms "real estate agent," "real estate salesperson," and "real estate broker" as synonyms. A real estate agent and a real estate salesperson are essentially the same, but a real estate broker is significantly different. Licensed real estate agents generally must work underneath a licensed broker. A broker can work on his or her own, or a broker can start a brokerage firm. A brokerage firm is a business structure where the licensed broker sponsors licensed real estate agents.

The broker-agent relationship is legally required. The specific requirements vary by state, so ensure that you understand the laws and rules that apply to you. A real estate broker often has significantly more professional experience as well as training than an agent. In some states, a real estate agent must work underneath a broker for a minimum number of years, take additional courses, and pass a more rigorous broker exam before he or she can obtain a broker's license.

Your real estate broker is responsible for reviewing all of the contracts and documents that you prepare on behalf of your clients. He or she will also ensure that you remain compliant with all regulations and laws. As a result, the real estate broker ultimately assumes liability for noncompliance.

The broker-agent relationship also often extends beyond this. Many brokers serve as mentors to their real estate agents. They may offer various perks to help real estate agents be more productive and profitable. At the same time, some brokers have requirements that their real estate agents must meet. With this in mind, you cannot assume that the first real estate broker who is interested in sponsoring you is the best one for you to work under.

The Importance of Interviewing Multiple Licensed Brokers

If you are like many other real estate agents, you initially wanted to sign on to work with the largest and most well-known brokerage firm in town. After all, this firm has name recognition and likely gets plenty of inbound leads for real estate agents to share. These large brokerage firms may be suitable for some real estate agents, but they may not be right for you.

Consider that some brokerage firms require their real estate agents to attend weekly or monthly meetings, meet quotas, host a specific number of open houses, and even man the phones for a specific amount of time each week. Other brokerage firms may not have any of these requirements, or they may have generally lenient expectations for these requirements.

Keep in mind that these requirements are not necessarily good or bad for all professionals. For example, new real estate agents may benefit from the structure, support, and camaraderie that comes from a regular meeting. They may appreciate the ability to generate leads from open houses and phone banks. Others, however, may find that these requirements interfere with how they want to run their operations as an independent contractor.

Real estate brokers and brokerage firms also offer different incentives and perks to their real estate agents. Some may pay for continuing education courses as well as some marketing materials. Some brokerage firms have on-site office space that you can share with other real estate agents, and others wholly require you to office out of your house. These are only a few of the many differences between brokers or brokerage firms, but perhaps the difference that most real estate agents are initially concerned with is the commission split. The most advantageous commission split may not always be the right one. It is important to look at the full requirements and perks in relation to the split.

What to Look for in a Broker

Before you start interviewing brokers, you may have specific expectations in mind. However, after you meet with a few brokers and tour various firms, your expectations could change dramatically. With this in mind, plan to sit down with at least three to five brokers before you make a firm commitment. Before a meeting, conduct due diligence by calling the firm's main number and by communicating with the broker by phone and email. The broker should be easy to reach, responsive, and friendly. While you will mostly be working on your own, you will need to be in regular communication with your broker. The receptionist should be professional and friendly as well.

When you visit the office, look at it through two sets of eyes. Initially, imagine yourself as a client who is arriving at the office to meet with you. Then, envision yourself working in this environment alongside the other real estate agents. The environment should be professional and inviting. It should also have all of the office equipment and other essentials that you need in order to be successful.

Your broker may allow you to create your own website as a real estate professional, but you will also have a presence on the broker's website. With this in mind, review the website carefully to ensure that it portrays an image that is suitable to you.

Important Questions to Ask before Making a Commitment

You can learn a lot about a broker before you sit down for an interview, but the interview is the time to get all of your important questions answered. You understandably want to go into the interview fully prepared with a list of questions. Here are questions that are relevant to most new real estate agents:

- Do you provide training for new real estate agents? What type of training is provided?
- Is mentorship required or available? What is the cost for mentorship? When can I meet with the person who will be mentoring me?
- What is your commission split? What additional fees and expenses will I be responsible for?
- What types of administrative services are included, and what services are available to me for a fee?
- What type of online presence is provided to real estate agents on the broker's website?

Can real estate agents have their own independent website?
- How many real estate agents work under the broker?
- What is the sales quota? What happens if the quota is not met?
- Will I be required to attend meetings or to man open houses and phone banks?
- Am I able to man open houses and phone banks if I want to use them for lead generation?
- Does the brokerage firm specialize in specific niches, such as investment property, listing services, or buyers' services?

After you speak with a few brokers and learn more about how their firms operate, you will clearly be able to determine what the right environment is for your specific needs and expectations. You can always move to another brokerage firm if you realize that you have not made the right initial choice. However, it is always best to do your due diligence and to get established with the right firm from the start.

Commission Splits – And When to Negotiate

When you meet with a real estate broker to discuss the commission-split structure, be aware that negotiating is often on the table even if the broker does not bring up the subject. As you negotiate, be aware of what you bring to the table as a new agent. Optimizing your income does not always mean optimizing your split. Focus on the training, services, and leads provided that can be essential as you are starting out.

Your Role as an Independent Contractor

The vast majority of real estate brokers sponsor real estate agents as independent contractors rather than as salaried employees. As an independent contractor, you are self-employed and are responsible for managing your business accordingly.

One of the most significant factors to remember as an independent contractor is that your broker is not responsible for your income tax liability. The commission that you receive will not have any taxes withheld. To avoid a large tax bill at the end of the year, make quarterly tax payments to the IRS. In some cases, you may be required to make these quarterly payments and could be penalized if you fail to make them.

As an independent contractor, you are able to offset your tax liability by writing off business-related expenses. For example, any office supplies that you purchase for business activities may be written off. Other common write-offs are for computers, related equipment and supplies, mileage, marketing that you pay for, a home office, and more. You must keep documentation for all write-offs. If you are audited by the IRS, you may be required to provide that documentation.

At first glance, this aspect of being an independent contractor can seem like a hassle. However, because of the many expenses that you are allowed to write off, you can dramatically reduce your tax liability and keep more of your income in your pocket. Consider keeping a file folder on your desk to collect receipts regularly. Log the expenses monthly so that you are not faced with an overwhelming task when you prepare your tax return at the end of the year.

The Day-To-Day

Location, Location, Location

Part of treating this like a career is to figure out how you are going to run your business—things like where are you going to work? Are you going to work in your brokerage's cubicle? Or would you prefer to work in a coffee shop? Nowadays, coworking is a popular option, and you could easily rent a space there for low cost. Of course, you can just work from home if that's an option for you. New agents will often be focused on having a really fancy office space to impress their clients. But do you know what would really impress her clients? Asking them where a convenient place to meet them would be. Is it at their home? Is it at a home that they want to tour? Or maybe it's at their local coffee shop. The chances that clients will want to go out of their way to meet at your office for something that can probably be done over a video conference or phone call is very low. So while your ego will feel great, I guarantee that your wallet will feel lighter and your clients will feel burdened.

Equipment

The next thing you need to figure out is your work equipment. Are you going to work primarily from a desktop or laptop computer, a tablet, or just from your cell phone? Speaking of cell phones, please set up your voicemail and remember to empty out your mailbox before it gets filled up. Clients and other agents will call you, and if for some reason you're not able to answer, they will not be able to leave you a voice message because your mailbox isn't set up or it's full. Nothing will lose you a lead and a potential client faster than being sent to voicemail and then not even being able to leave a voicemail. You're also going to need a printer. You will probably want to print out listings from the MLS, other types of reports, and presentations that you might give to your clients. An alternative to this is to just rely on printing services like FedEx or your local print shop. How about a scanner? Nowadays our mobile devices often replace what a scanner does, but to be honest, it's not as good, so if you want to be the best, it's best to invest in a decent scanner—one with a copier function combined is even better.

What to Wear

Have you figured out what you're going to wear to work? Part of it depends on your persona and personality. The other aspect depends on your marketplace. Either way, you want to make sure that you are true to yourself, that you are comfortable, and that you look professional. In some areas, looking professional means wearing a suit and tie. But someone wearing a suit and tie to show homes on Redondo Beach might look kind of silly.

What Are You Actually Doing?

How about your job description? What kind of real estate do you want to do? Do you only want to sell luxury properties? Maybe you want to be the top leasing agent in your area. You'll need to decide what types of property you are willing to work with and when you would rather refer deals out to other agents (more on that later). Part of being successful in real estate is knowing what you're good at and then doing more of that and outsourcing things that you are not good at.

When Do You Work?

What are your working hours? Do you want to be reachable 24/7? I actually recommend that for newer agents as a way to stand out and differentiate themselves from the competition. But if you are not interested in being reachable 24/7 or your life currently doesn't afford you that opportunity, then you need to decide what hours you are going to work. Be clear about those hours upfront with all of your clients so that if your hours are nine to five and your client reaches out at 5:30 they won't be expecting you to respond right away. Setting expectations is really important, and setting expectations with your working hours is the most basic step you can take.

Startup Costs

This is a business. There are costs to starting any business. Fortunately, the costs to get started in real estate are among the lowest out of any other business, but they still exist and you should be prepared for those costs. It is okay to be frugal and to be careful with the way you spend your money, but it's another thing to refuse to invest in your own business. If you don't even believe in your business enough to invest in it, then how will you be able to show confidence to your clients?

Budgeting for Success

Let's go over some of the costs that are involved with getting started in the real estate industry. We already talked about some of the work equipment that you are going to need, like a computer or a cell phone and maybe a printer and a scanner. Some of those things come with monthly fees.

> **Side Note**: Are you prepared to make little to nothing for 18 months? Because that's how long it could take until you make your first sale; hopefully you do it much sooner, and by reading this book, your chances that you will are significantly higher.

Ideally you have some money set aside for your own living expenses for at least nine months, but ideally 12 months. If you are spending your last few dollars on your real estate exam and license fee, then you are going to have a very difficult time gaining traction to be successful in this business. It would be much better for you to set money aside regularly and save up before deciding to start off on this new business venture of becoming a real estate agent.

The vast majority of brokerage firms that you will consider joining are going to require you and all other agents to be members of the National Association of Realtors, a trade organization that represents the business interests of real estate agents and brokers. There are costs associated with membership, including sign-up fees, local dues, state dues, and national dues, among others. Aside from the sign-up fees, you will pay the rest of the fees every year to maintain membership in the National Association of Realtors. These costs can typically range between $300 and $900.

You will also be responsible for the cost of your own MLS subscription. The MLS subscription is required for you to list homes for sale and for you to browse homes that are already listed for sale. Your MLS fees are also paid annually (sometimes quarterly or semi-annually), and they typically include a first-time sign-up fee. The annual fee can range from $200 to $1,000.

Then there are other costs, like signs (open house, for sale, for lease) and business cards.

> **Key Tip**: Business cards: YES - Buy the business cards. Signs: NO - Don't buy the signs yet. Wait until there is a need. As you can see, there are a lot of costs associated with getting started in real estate. Being able to cut costs and save money where you can is vital. Chances are, you won't need real estate signs for at least several months into your real estate career. So why not save that money for things you need right now and then

purchase the signs when the need arises? You can usually have signs made and shipped to you in just a few days, and you almost always have that much lead time before you will need the signs.

Another quick note about business cards. You will want to decide whether you want to add your headshot to the business card or not. You will find that it is not uncommon for real estate agents to include a photo of their face on business cards. Honestly, this is kind of unusual compared to other industries. You do not normally see lawyers and doctors with their photographs on their business cards. The face is an easier way for clients to remember you instead of with a name on a card only. You will have to decide which you prefer. Maybe you have some cards printed with your photograph and others without.

Some other costs to be aware of in real estate are gasoline and car maintenance, especially when working with buyer clients who you are going to be showing homes all over, covering lots of mileage. Also there is the cost of marketing a home for sale, like photos (because you are definitely not taking the photos yourself on your cell phone, I know that for sure), cleaning, and having brochures or postcards printed.

Needless to say, this is not a definitive or exhaustive list of all the startup costs you are going to encounter as you launch your real estate business. But this should give you an idea of some of the larger and most important expenses, as well as some ways to save money for things you do need instead of spending it on things that you do not need.

5

Why Clients Choose Agents

When trying to understand why clients choose to work with a particular agent, it is imperative to put yourself in the clients' shoes. There are a wide range of marketing and outreach techniques that you can utilize, such as canvassing your market with fliers or mailers, fielding calls on your brokerage firm's phone bank, standing in at open houses for other agents, and more. However, getting in front of potential clients is only the first step in the client-attraction process. You also must actively appeal to them in specific ways that address their wants, needs, and concerns.

The Strength of Your Broker's Clout

Many real estate agents believe that working under a reputable, established brokerage company will give them a competitive edge. However, when today's buyers and sellers look for an agent, they often do not call a specific brokerage firm that they are familiar with and ask to be assigned to the next available agent. Instead, they may ask friends and family members for recommendations or work with a real estate agent who they already know and trust. Others may interview several real estate agents until they find the right professional for them, and an agent's broker may never be taken into consideration.

Some buyers and sellers will go through most or all of the transaction without knowing which broker their real estate agent works with. Because of this, you cannot rely on the strength of your brokerage firm's clout as a client recruitment tool. Working under the right brokerage company is nonetheless crucial to your professional success for a variety of other reasons. The commission split, the culture, the support and services available, and more will all impact your success and profitability as a real estate agent.

Refining Your Approach

When it comes to obtaining new clients, getting in front of potential clients is only half the battle. Refining your approach so that your initial message is optimized for effectiveness is important, but be aware that there is not a catch-all, foolproof approach that you can fall back on. Instead, you must be aware of your own strengths and weaknesses. You also must recognize that the different expectations, wants, and needs of different home buyers and sellers will impact their perception of your strengths and weaknesses. With this in mind, you can see that you cannot please everyone.

While each real estate agent is an individual, there are several general personality types that most real estate agents closely identify with. Potential clients often intentionally or subconsciously search for a real estate agent with a personality type that is most appealing to them. By understanding what these personality types are and which type or types you associate with, you can tailor your approach and your marketing message to appeal to the right potential clients. What are the general personality types?

The Fun Person

All successful real estate agents must be personable and professional, but some take this a step further by injecting their own fun personality into the equation. These real estate agents have the ability to transform what may be a stressful experience for their clients into a more enjoyable experience through their approach. They are consistently straight-shooters, but they may incorporate humor or other light-hearted elements into all aspects of the service that they provide.

Real estate agents communicate with other agents as well as vendors throughout a typical transaction as well, but some clients may not see these interactions between their real estate agent and other parties until later in the process. However, through referrals and other factors, some potential clients may be aware of the positive impact that a fun personality can have on all parties involved in their transaction. For example, injecting humor into a stressful situation may defuse the tension and help to bring the parties together.

The Smart Expert

Even a relatively smooth real estate transaction can have complexities that require professional expertise. Through licensing standards, all real estate agents have the same basic knowledge. However, some have extensive expertise in a refined niche that may be relevant to specific buyers and sellers. Buyers and sellers who are dealing with unique circumstances often recognize the need for professional expertise. They are uncertain about various requirements, nuances, and more, and they want to find a smart expert who can guide them every step of the way.

The smart expert may also be an appealing personality type to inexperienced buyers and sellers. For many people, the purchase and sale of a home are among the most significant transactions that they will make throughout their lifetime. They understand that their finances and other critical aspects of their lives are directly tied up in the transaction in front of them. By choosing to work with an expert-level real estate agent, they may feel more confident as they make critical decisions that they may otherwise be fairly confused or indecisive about.

The Suave Negotiator

Most real estate transactions involve some degree of negotiations, so all real estate agents should have excellent negotiating skills. However, when clients are going into a transaction with very specific expectations or with special circumstances, the need for a suave negotiator increases substantially. These unique situations may be related to the seller's need for a specific sales price to pay off a high mortgage balance, a buyer's or seller's need to negotiate for repairs based on property condition and more. In a competitive market, a real estate agent with exceptional negotiation skills will be in high demand.

Some buyers and sellers who are walking into a transaction without known special circumstances may also prefer to work with a suave negotiator. For example, clients who want to get a great deal on their purchase or sale may be particularly drawn to a real estate agent with stellar negotiation skills.

The Calming Presence

The last personality trait that is common among real estate agents is a calm demeanor. These individuals immediately put their clients at ease, and their calming effect can extend to others involved in the transaction as well. When dealing with an emotional or passionate client, the real estate agent's ability to diffuse tense or stressful situations with innate personality traits is a true gift.

Buyers and sellers who are drawn to real estate agents with a calming presence may be those who have a low tolerance for stress or who have a passionate spouse who will be involved in the transaction. In some cases, buyers and sellers who feel intimidated and anxious about different aspects of the process may appreciate a real estate agent with the ability to ease their mind.

A Blend of Personalities

While many real estate agents will strongly relate to one of these personality types, some may discover that they represent a blend of two or even three personalities. For example, a smart expert may also be a keen negotiator. As you decide which of these personality types best describe you, keep in mind that you also must consider the clients' perception. Your initial presentation during a first meeting, in an initial phone call, or even via marketing material will impact a person's interest in choosing you as his or her real estate agent.

According to the National Association of Realtors' 2020 Profile of Home Buyers and Sellers, 73 percent of homebuyers interviewed only a single real estate agent before deciding which agent to work with. This does not necessarily mean that they are not discerning and will accept the first real estate agent who they come in contact with. Instead, it may mean that they strongly pay attention to messaging in marketing materials and in online profiles.

It also may indicate that potential clients rely heavily on personal referrals. When a previous client tells a friend or family member about the great experience that they had working with you, they will likely provide specific details about that experience. Through these details, the potential new client will be able to

determine if you are the type of real est
that he or she is searching for.

The Impact on Your Career

As a busy and successful real estate agent, you understandably want to find great clients to serve. When you showcase your personality upfront, you will attract clients who are drawn to the experience that you provide. The typical real estate sales transaction can last for several months in some cases. Finding clients that you gel with impacts your ability to provide them with great service. It sets the stage for a less stressful and more productive experience for all parties involved.

In turn, this impacts the type of reviews that your clients provide after the sale is finalized. How important is this to your future income potential? According to the NAR study, 91 percent of home buyers state that they plan to use their real estate agent for their future transactions and will recommend their real estate agent to others.

The Experience That New Clients Are Looking For

Real estate buyers understand that real estate agents do more than open the doors to listed homes and prepare sales contracts. Likewise, sellers know that their real estate agents do more than plant a sign in the front yard. The processes of buying and selling a home are both exciting and intimidating for many people. Concerns about finding the right home in a great area and getting a fair deal on that home are common in buyers. Sellers generally want to find a qualified buyer as soon as possible who is willing to pay close to or more than the asking price. These are lofty goals that often cause buyers and sellers a considerable amount of anxiety.

With so many real estate agents vying for each client's attention, how can you let your experience shine through? Based on your personality type or types, consider the clients you are more likely to attract and to gel with. Think about what their common hot buttons are, such as if they need an agent with extensive experience as a negotiator. Identify the skills and professional experiences that you bring to the table, and highlight these attributes prominently in your marketing material.

For example, on your professional bio, go beyond mentioning your years of experience and your sales stats. Provide specific details that your target clients may find most prevalent. When you speak with potential clients initially, find or create opportunities in your dialog to draw attention to your key selling points as a real estate agent.

Some real estate agents believe that homing in on specific strengths and targeting a specific client base may unnecessarily limit their ability to connect with more clients. In reality, there are enough clients to go around. You may increase your appeal to the specific clients who you may click best with when you highlight your personality type in combination with your unique skills and professional experience.

By doing so, you may win more clients even though you are tailoring your marketing approach.

How to Stand Out and Let Your Strengths Shine

Many buyers and sellers are uncertain about how to select a real estate agent, so they understandably ask for referrals from friends and family members. Many people also personally know real estate agents and may be inclined to work with people they know and trust. In reality, however, experience, skills, and personality types trump familiarity when it comes to finding the best real estate agent for the job. With this in mind, how can you earn a client's business over a real estate agent they are familiar with?

In marketing material and in person, self-promotion is key. Do not worry about coming off as too arrogant or bold. In a strong sense, you are selling yourself to potential clients. Touting your strengths and providing personalized details about how those strengths will benefit the specific client's needs and concerns are essential. The real estate agent who a potential client is familiar with has an edge over you in the areas of rapport and trust, so it is essential that you establish a solid connection with potential clients from the start.

More than that, showcase the exceptional customer service that you will provide. Treat initial communications with a potential client as a job interview. After all, that is exactly what this stage in your relationship with a new client is. Everything from being personable, attentive, and knowledgeable to responding promptly and addressing specific concerns are crucial.

Understanding why buyers and sellers choose one specific real estate agent over another is vital. It enables you to look at the process from a potential client's point of view. By doing so, you can adjust your approach and can ultimately improve your ability to connect with new clients and to earn their business.

6

Creating and Managing Your Online Presence

Unless or until your real estate business is driven solely by referral business, you must rely on marketing to drive leads. As a result, your income as a real estate agent is substantially influenced by your ability to generate quality leads. Both buyers and sellers will use digital media to research real estate agents. Because marketing drives the cycle, you need to focus heavily on controlling what potential clients discover about you online and developing an excellent online marketing campaign that effectively generates leads.

Understanding Your Digital Footprint

When a potential client searches for your name online, you want him or her to find a full array of professional marketing material that positions you as a true expert. However, is this really what potential clients will find? If you have not conducted an online search of your name recently, now is the time to do so.

Your digital footprint may be far more expansive than your initial assumption. A Google query could reveal tweets, Facebook posts, personal photos that you shared on a private website, and more. This may be information that you posted personally, but it can impact your professional reputation.

Keep in mind that your digital footprint extends beyond what you post online and on social media platforms. Your name may show up in searches if you have appeared in news stories or articles, if you have been involved in a lawsuit, and for many other reasons. Even if negative press covers events that occurred many years ago, the online content can still haunt you as a professional today.

Improving Your Online Reputation

In many cases, removing information from the internet once it has been posted is difficult to do. You can pursue a legal route in some situations. For tidbits, stories, posts, and images that will find a permanent place online, however, a reasonable strategy is to bury the negative press with positive press. After all, most people will gather all of the facts that they need to know about you on the first page or two of Google search results.

How can you improve your online reputation using this strategy? Initially, you can focus on publishing content that presents you more favorably. Getting this content to rank above other content can be challenging, so learn the basics of search engine optimization. Consider getting other reputable websites to publish a professional bio or a personal interest story about you. Your broker's website could be a great place to start. You can get involved in community or social awareness events that may be publicized online as well.

If you do not already have your own professional website, now is the time to create one. Your broker likely will post a bio page that may show up in search engine rankings, and your professional website can also take a prime spot in search results.

It can take many months to stifle negative online press with positive, professional information about you. However, your efforts will ultimately be instrumental in your ability to attract new clients.

Protecting and Managing Your Online Reputation

Simply improving your online reputation is not enough. Your potential clients will continue to use the internet to learn more about you. To protect your online reputation from additional damage, monitor what you post on social media platforms carefully. Ensure that your network of friends and family on social media do their part to keep undesirable information about you off of the internet.

Keep in mind that your clients and other people can also post information about you online going forward. For example, an unhappy client can leave a negative review on a third-party review website. Legal issues in your personal life can also crop up online at any time. Doing your best to provide excellent service to each of your clients and being an upstanding citizen will be keys to reducing the chance of negative information being reported about you. You should continue to run a Google query on your name periodically so that you are always on top of your online reputation.

The Need for a Professional Website

The importance of having a professional website goes beyond its impact on reputation management. All real estate agents generally have a small bio on a broker's website. A true professional, however, has a dedicated website that is loaded with resources for buyers and sellers. As a valuable resource, the website may be bookmarked so that potential or established clients can continue using it for their various needs. This keeps your name at the front of their mind, and it also positions you as a helpful, knowledgeable expert in your field.

A professional website is a critical component for lead generation, branding, online reputation, and more. It is far more robust than the simple bio page that your broker may create for you. Furthermore, you control the scope of the message on your website. To maximize your website's reach and benefits, ensure that each page is fully optimized based on SEO techniques. Then, publish regular blog posts on your website.

A nice-looking website gives you another location to showcase listings and to generate interest in those listings and in your services. By using various website tools, you can collect visitors' contact info for an opt-in email campaign. Through an email campaign, you can stay in touch with your clients and continue to show off your expertise by linking to your blog posts, announcing closed transactions, and more.

Your website enables you to have full control over your professional brand and public image. This is not always easy to express in a short bio on a broker's website. Through branding, you establish expectations about the services that you provide, and you can attract clients who you may work well with based on needs and personality types.

How to Generate Website Leads

While some people will specifically search for your name as a professional real estate agent or will type in your website's URL, many others will stumble upon your information through various online marketing methods. Because of this, your ability to drive traffic to your website is essential in order to generate leads from your website.

Search engine optimization generally will not produce immediate results, but the effort will pay off over time. It can take several weeks or longer for search engine bots to crawl over your website and to use collected data for ranking purposes. SEO techniques are used to improve your website's visibility to search engines for relevant searches. However, simply being visible is not enough. The search engines must also determine that your website will meet the users' needs based on the searched words or phrases.

At one time, trying to manipulate online content to bolster your website's placement on search engine results pages was effective. Today's search engines, however, are fine-tuned to penalize those who try to manipulate the system. With this in mind, a beginner's approach to search engine optimization is to create a website that is truly useful to your target audience. In the process, you may naturally incorporate a variety of related keywords into your text, and you may generate excellent content that lays the foundation for backlinks and other SEO essentials.

Blog posts that are written with your target audience in mind are also an essential part of a real estate agent's SEO campaign. Regular posts keep content on your website fresh, and this is a key factor that plays into your search engine rankings. More than that, however, is the fact that blog posts provide your visitors with truly useful content. In order to turn your website into a lead generation machine, you need to bring visitors to the website through the creation of content that they actually want to read. Ideally, this will also be content that they feel inspired to share with others. When the content motivates them to take action, they may contact you directly for a consultation or opt in to receive your email newsletter.

Of course, having a website with a blog will not necessarily generate an ample supply of leads initially. You will need to actively promote your website, and there are a few methods to do this. Social media marketing is generally free and effective. Simply post links to your blog posts regularly on your social media pages. Encourage your followers to share the content. If funds allow, you can take advantage of paid advertising, such as pay-per-click or social media advertising.

Over time, you will grow a healthy database of established and potential clients who have opted in to receive your marketing material. You can directly email them a link to your blog posts and to a newsletter regularly. At the same time, your followers on social media accounts will grow. As a result, the links you post to your blog posts and other online content will receive more traffic over time.

How to Convert Website Leads

The unfortunate reality is that having a huge email distribution list and a ton of social media followers will not necessarily make you as busy and as successful as you want to be. You must be effective at converting online leads into clients. How can you improve in this area?

The real estate industry revolves around people and personal relationships. Your clients have strong attachments to the homes that they are selling, and they have equally strong sentiments about homes that they are preparing to buy. Clients want to work with a real estate agent who understands their wants and needs. When you initially communicate with a client, take time to get to know those wants and needs. Then, repeat those wants and needs back to the client so that they are aware of your deep understanding. From there, present how you intent to help them achieve their goals and why you are the right real estate agent for them.

As important as it is to connect personally with potential clients as soon as possible, you also must showcase that you are a true professional who is devoted to serving your clients. Maintain accessibility and provide prompt follow-up. Always follow through on what you say you are going to do in a timely manner. Remember that the client is interviewing you and assessing your ability to help them from the first interaction.

A single satisfied client is a truly valuable resource. This is a client who may turn to you for future needs. Considering that many people buy and sell homes every few years, building a long list of satisfied clients is essential to growing your business. More than that, this client can refer many other potential clients to you. Taking the time to truly nurture all website leads from the initial contact can yield tremendous returns over time.

Using YouTube Videos for Marketing

YouTube is often overlooked as an effective marketing platform, but YouTube videos can have a powerful effect on both your website's search engine rankings and on your professional image. Everybody has heard the saying about a picture being worth a thousand words. A video adds motion, sound, and other elements to the mix. Because YouTube is both a platform and a search engine, your YouTube videos can actually drive traffic to your website. Your videos can also be posted on social media platforms like Twitter and Facebook. These same videos can be posted on your website as a vlog or in combination with your blog to highlight client experiences and more.

The complicated search engine algorithms take into account the number and quality of inbound links to your website when determining rankings, so YouTube videos can bolster your website's ranking on search engine results pages. In addition, the videos themselves can show up in search results. This increases your visibility online. When you are trying to improve your professional image and push back negative press on search engine results pages, your videos can play an instrumental role.

Of course, your videos' content can also be invaluable to your professional image. You could create a video bio of yourself to post on your website. This can serve as a brief introduction to prospective clients. Because it is far more personal than words on a screen, a video bio can be powerful. Your videos can be used to highlight tips for buyers and sellers and to otherwise back up your blog posts, offer essential insights, and more. When your videos are used in these ways, you showcase yourself as a true expert in the real estate industry. At the same time, your website's status as a valuable resource is elevated. This could lead to more bookmarks, shares, and repeat visitors.

Why Is Social Media Important to Real Estate Agents?

Simply having a professional website is not enough. Even if your website ranks well in search engine results, you need to optimize your visibility as a real estate agent in other ways. Often, self-promotion is a major driver of traffic to a real estate agent's website. Social media plays a direct role in both of these areas.

By posting regularly on social media platforms, you are increasing your visibility to those within your circle and to others who find your content. Your posts and pages can directly send traffic to your website. At the same time, creating truly useful posts can lead to shares and can highlight your expertise in your field. If you have not yet established a professional presence on Facebook, Instagram, and Twitter, now is the perfect time to do so.

Facebook

Facebook enables you to create a page for your business. This allows you to maintain a personal profile that is separate from your professional content. However, you can and should ask friends and family to follow your business profile and to share it with others. On the business profile page, you will post your links to blog posts, professional videos, and any other content that your followers may find valuable.

You can promote your posts on your business space. If you choose to pay for this marketing, ensure that you take full advantage of the audience customization features. Real estate agents serve a specific geographic area, so you only want to pay to market your content on Facebook to those who are within this geographic area.

Twitter and Instagram

On both Twitter and Instagram, you can create entirely new profiles for your business presence. By posting content with strategically selected hashtags, you can increase traffic and visibility. You can also encourage retweets on Twitter. While images and videos can and should be used on Facebook and Twitter, these elements are essential on Instagram. Ensure that you post high-quality images and videos.

While social media platforms can and should be used to drive traffic to your website, you also should use your website to build your following on social media platforms. In fact, on your website as well as on your business cards, emails, and all other content that established and potential clients will see, include links to all of your online presences. This will ultimately increase your exposure and visibility.

Pulling It All Together

If you are a new real estate agent and you are building your online presence from scratch, the effort should always start with defining what your online reputation is currently and what image you want to portray. Then, create a detailed list of all of the prep work that you need to do, such as by creating professional presences on social media platforms.

From that point, it is a matter of creating excellent content. You can and should start off a blog and new social media accounts with three to five quality posts. This ensures that you are offering your followers and visitors useful content right away. Then, create a marketing calendar that lays the foundation for publishing content on your blog and social media platforms on a regular basis.

7

Zillow, iBuyers, and Other Threats

According to some sources, as many as 80 percent of new real estate agents throw in the towel during their first year. Many others will follow suit in the subsequent years. There are many reasons why some real estate agents do not persevere and reach the high level of success that they initially planned on. For example, unreasonable expectations about workload, a poor marketing plan, and inadequate funding are serious obstacles for many new real estate agents. Regardless of whether it is your first year in the business or you have been trying to grow your business for many years, there are other economic and market challenges at play as well.

As is the case with most hurdles that you will face in your professional career, knowledge and preparation are keys to navigating bumpy waters successfully. With this in mind, what are some of the most pressing obstacles that today's real estate agents are facing or will soon face? More than that, how can you strategically prepare for them?

An Economic Downturn

Thanks to the COVID-19 pandemic and a variety of other factors that culminated into a perfect storm, the economy has been sluggish in recent years. The housing market, on the other hand, has been booming in most areas of the country. Interest rates continue to be close to historic lows, and these rates have been mostly in place for more than a decade. Millennials, who have been sitting on the sidelines as renters for years, are entering the market in droves. At the same time, inventory is relatively low. These factors have all combined to create a housing market that remains strong and active. In fact, housing prices in many areas of the country are rapidly rising as a result.

This has caused some people to worry about the possibility of a housing bubble and a potential crash. Because the heat in the market is rooted in fundamentals rather than on prospecting, many economic experts do not believe that a crash is imminent.

On the other hand, the real estate market is cyclical, and we are clearly at the peak of the cycle currently. At this point, new construction is booming to keep pace with demand. However, over time, we will enter a stage known as hyper-supply. During this stage in the cycle, construction catches up to and even passes demand. As construction continues, the market enters a recession.

Historically, this cycle is 18 years long, but this is an average rather than a hard-and-fast rule. Given the fact that the last major housing market recession started in 2007, it is clear that a market downturn is in the future. It may not happen this year, but it likely will happen at some point in the next few years.

Preparing for the Next Market Dip

Given the almost certainty of a real estate market dip within the next few years, now is the time to prepare your business and your finances for this eventuality. It is easy to have a general feeling that the good times will go on forever. The large commission checks are rolling in now. Between your income and your steady workload, planning for a rainy day may be at the back of your mind. However, the best time to prepare for rainy weather is when the sun is shining.

If you do not currently do so, set aside a chunk of each commission check you receive for that proverbial rainy day. Commissions will be few and far between during the next downturn. This is money that you can rely on to continue marketing and to remain afloat until business picks up again.

Now is also a great time to build your business. When real estate agents are very busy serving clients, practical matters like developing a client list and nurturing relationships can fall by the wayside. However, repeat clients and referral business can keep your business afloat when new leads dry up. You can use lead capture resources to build a database of new leads. You also should provide stellar customer service to established clients. Continue to stay in touch after deals close, and always ask for referrals.

This is also a great time to develop name recognition. Focus heavily on marketing in a specific geographic area. When people in that area plan to buy or sell in the years ahead, you want your name to pop into their heads. You may not always get business from them, but you may at least be given the chance to make your pitch. If you are not on the doorstep when a potential client is ready to make a decision, you will likely miss out on the opportunity to earn business.

Keep in mind that a market downturn does not mean that business activities have stopped. People will always need to buy and sell homes. However, with diminished activity compared to boom times, competition will be fierce. By building your business now and by ensuring that you continue to have a marketing budget through dry spells, you can work your way through the downturn and into the next boom.

Increasing Mortgage Interest Rates

Mortgage interest rates took a dramatic dip during the start of the last recession. While they have bobbled slightly since that time, they are now on a slow and steady climb upward. Because the Fed moderates interest rates, it is not reasonable to expect mortgage rates to shoot up overnight or even at a perilous pace. However, as they continue to slowly edge upward, you will see increasing pressure on the housing market.

According to the National Association of Realtors, approximately 86 percent of home buyers use a home loan to finance their purchases. With this in mind, changes to interest rates can play a dramatic role in your business activities as a real estate agent. Specifically, a home mortgage payment is derived from three basic factors. These are the principal loan balance, the interest rate and the term. The principal loan balance is a factor of the property's sales price and the buyer's down payment amount.

As interest rates rise, some buyers will be required to make a larger down payment to buy the same house. Because of this, they may need to save up for a longer period of time before entering the market. Other buyers may simply decide to buy a smaller and more affordable house. Still others may decide that renting is a better option for them.

You can see that increasing mortgage interest rates alone will impact your business dramatically. However, keep in mind that housing prices in many areas are skyrocketing as well. As interest rates continue to rise and as housing prices rise, more buyers will be forced to sit on the sidelines temporarily or indefinitely. From your perspective as a real estate agent, this means that your pool of potential buyers will shrink.

Adjusting for Rising Interest Rates

Regardless of the market that you work in, there will always be real estate buyers and sellers. Nonetheless, it makes sense to cast your line in an area where the fish are more plentiful. With this in mind, it is important to consider what will happen to your specific market as interest rates rise. Each geographic location has its own factors to consider. However, generally, you will find that people migrate slowly from expensive urban hubs to more affordable suburban locations.

Because of this, consider targeting outlying areas that have high growth potential right now. These may be more affordable areas that are close to commuter transportation systems or new areas of commercial growth. Become an expert in these micro-communities or neighborhoods. By building your business in these areas now, you will be one step ahead of the competition when these areas are in higher demand in the near future.

Low Inventory

In early 2021, news about a pandemic-related lumber shortage gave the housing market an unexpected challenge. The shortage caused the price of new homes to skyrocket, and this had a trickle-down effect on established homes listed for sale. On top of that, the lumber shortage caused builders to slow or even to temporarily halt new starts. This added to the stress on the housing market and caused housing prices to climb higher.

Because new construction sales had slowed, there was an uptick in the sale of established homes. The available inventory of homes on the market in many areas dried up. In fact, in some areas, bidding wars became commonplace.

While the stress on the market has eased slightly since its peak, this unexpected turn of events was a solid reminder of how vulnerable the market is. More than that, it also reminded real estate agents that factors like labor shortages, shutdowns in other sectors of the economy, and other issues can trickle over to the real estate market and can have a devastating impact as a result. It was impossible to predict the COVID-19 pandemic and its far-reaching effects, and that is exactly why real estate agents need to be prepared to deal with unexpected issues at a moment's notice.

Preparing for Low Inventory in the Future

Regardless of how well-established you are as a real estate agent, you cannot sell homes if owners are not listing them for sale. New real estate agents, however, may be particularly vulnerable to a low-inventory environment. After all, established real estate agents may have a firm financial buffer established. They may also derive extensive business from referrals and from established clients. This means that the few transactions that do develop in a low-inventory environment may be more likely to be absorbed by established real estate agents rather than by new agents.

What can you do today to prepare for a sudden and unexpected shortage in inventory? When inventory is low, sellers often expect their homes to sell for top dollar or even to be the focus of a bidding war. Because of their high expectations, they often want to work with a real estate agent who they know and trust or a real estate agent who has been around the proverbial block. If you are a new real estate agent, you understandably do not have either of these attributes working for you.

It takes time to accumulate experience and to build a solid network of established clients that you can draw referrals and repeat business from. The best time to focus on these critical elements is now, while the market is hot. Consider how you can leverage the benefit of each closed deal. In addition to asking for referrals and establishing a follow-up relationship with the client, build your social media marketing efforts. Showcase your listings or closings. Ask your followers to share your posts. Send direct mailers out announcing closed transactions in the neighborhood. The more steps that you can take now to position yourself as an experienced, successful expert, the easier it will be to earn business down the road when listings are thin.

Online Listing Portals

Zillow, Redfin, and other online listing portals have become increasingly popular among homebuyers, and they have changed the way many people search for homes. Consider a few decades ago, before their prevalence. Prospective buyers would spend time driving around through neighborhoods they were interested in with the hope of finding a beautiful house that appealed to them. When they found such a house, they would contact the listing agent to schedule a tour. If that particular listing did not suit them, the real estate agent would have a new buying client to work with. At that point, the real estate agent could take a hands-on role in the search process.

Today, however, many prospective buyers prefer to spend hours searching through Zillow, Redfin, and other platforms on their own. Through these platforms, they can look at dozens of photos, read property descriptions, learn about schools, estimate their mortgage payment, and more.

Of course, these online listing portals have not completely erased the job of a real estate agent. After all, at some point, buyers will connect with a real estate agent for a home tour and will get on the agent's radar. Because this point is reached much later in the process, however, the real estate agent's role in the process is increasingly limited. There is less time to establish rapport, to showcase your expertise, and to earn future business.

More than that, prospective buyers are generally reaching out to real estate agents through online listing portals. This means that they are decreasingly asking their friends, family members, and neighbors for referrals.

Working Alongside Online Listing Portals

Online listing portals are here to stay for the time being, so savvy real estate agents must learn how to thrive while working alongside them. The good news is that there are a number of strategies that you can use to get in front of prospective clients earlier in the process.

One strategy is to create a dedicated neighborhood website for each community that you focus on. Include relevant information for homeowners, such as stories or stats related to property developments nearby, property tax rates, traffic stats, and more. It will take ample time to keep the website updated and relevant. However, when you build a solid following on your website, you are positioned as a community expert in their eyes. These are individuals who know and hopefully trust you before they even think about selling or buying real estate. When the time comes for them to select a real estate agent, they may prefer to hire you rather than to work with a random individual who they stumble across on an online listing portal.

While this may be one of the more effective ways to tackle the challenge of online listing portals, there are other strategies to consider as well. For example, if you are less tech-savvy, you can create a monthly neighborhood newsletter or even send an email blast to a targeted group of individuals. You may also strategically work yourself into a neighborhood's online forum or social media group, if permitted. Keep in mind that your goal is to get in front of homeowners before they decide to list their home and buy a new home. Your goal should also include a way to showcase your expertise in the real estate market and your focus on their community.

iBuyers

Each listing that you have as a real estate agent gives you the opportunity to earn a commission. More than that, it enables you to advertise your business with a yard sign and other marketing efforts. You can also derive business from online listing platforms that your listing is displayed on. After the closing, the possibilities for referral and repeat business add to the benefits.

Unfortunately, many homeowners are choosing to sell their home to an iBuyer rather than to proceed with the traditional method of selling a home. An iBuyer, such as Opendoor, Offerpad, or Zillow Offers, makes an instant cash offer on a home in its current condition. To the seller, it presents a hassle-free way to sell a house in its current condition. There are no stressful negotiations, concerns about a buyer's financing falling through, or other unfortunately common scenarios associated with selling a house.

If you have not already lost at least some business to an iBuyer, there is a solid chance that you will at some point in the future. While the impact on your present-day income can be tremendous, iBuyer platforms also reduce your ability to build your business over time.

Competing with iBuyers

There are two primary opportunities for you to position yourself strategically against iBuyers. First, it is important to define what your selling points are as a real estate agent. iBuyers offer a fast, hassle-free solution, but they often leave money on the table. Generally, a seller will not get the best offer possible unless they list their home on the open market. There are instances when this is strategic for a seller, such as if the seller needs to move out quickly and does not want to be hassled by home tours and fixing up the house. However, many sellers have a lot of money invested in their house, and they do not want to throw money away unnecessarily.

With this in mind, you bring the opportunity to list the home on the open market and to potentially get a better sales price. At the time same, you can showcase your expertise as being instrumental in optimizing the final sales price and the time on the market. Because of your expertise, the sellers could potentially have less stressful and more successful negotiations, fewer home tours before an offer is received, and other essential benefits.

Now that you know what your selling points are over an iBuyer, you can identify the two opportunities for showcasing those benefits. You can directly market yourself as a preferred option over an iBuyer through social media marketing, direct-mail marketing, and more. These are opportunities to get in front of a seller before the individual has even decided to list the home. Educating the homeowner about the advantages you offer in comparison to an iBuyer can be a slow, steady process that starts today.

The other opportunity is when a seller is preparing to list the home for sale. A homeowner, for example, may request a consultation with you and may also get a quote from an iBuyer. Your comparative market analysis will be a huge selling point in this situation. It gives the buyer greater insight into what the home could actually be worth when it is listed on the open market and how long it could take to sell the home. Before the seller has this relatively firm information based on actual market stats, his or her imagination in these areas can run wild. By providing firm facts, you eliminate the gray area.

More than that, your CMA presentation gives you the chance to showcase your market expertise. Selling a house can seem like a hassle upfront, but the right real estate agent can simplify the process. This may also be a great time to answer questions about the types of fixes required before listing the home. Often, homes do not need quite as much repair efforts as a homeowner initially assumes.

Increased Government Regulation

Government regulations play their role in the housing market, and a growing number of regulations can mean increasing headaches for real estate agents. According to the National Association of Home Builders, approximately 23.8 percent of the average cost of a new single-family home built in 2021 was attributed to regulations. This includes regulations at the development and the construction phases. This represents a 10.9 percent increase from 2016.

In addition to these regulations, other regulations at local levels often limit the number and types of homes that can be built in that specific area. The impact of these two factors means that government has a direct and significant role in both housing prices and supply. These are the two factors that are directly decreasing the affordability of homes across the country.

As a real estate agent, the affordability of housing directly impacts your profitability. While higher sales prices mean higher commission checks, they also can make it increasingly difficult for you to match buyers with homes listed on the market. On a larger scale, these factors can drive the market into its cyclical downturns at a faster pace and could make it more challenging to dig out of market recessions. Because there is an upward trend on government regulations, these are serious factors to pay attention to going forward.

Confronting Government Regulations

There are a number of steps that you can take to get involved with government policy-making. For example, you can join and participate in industry groups. These include the NAR and your state-level realtor association. There are also groups that focus on the construction industry, the residential housing industry, financing, and more that may be lobbying on your behalf.

Pay attention to industry news so that you can make informed decisions as a voter. Consider the benefits of donating your money and time to various lobbies as well. Getting involved and spreading the word are essential ways for you to make a difference at the grassroots level.

While you understandably want to lobby against unnecessary regulations, you also must prepare for the possibility that the trend will continue. Because increasing regulations may yield greater pressure on the balance between supply, demand, and pricing, you need to understand how pending regulations can impact your business. Networking with your fellow real estate agents and joining online forums are great ways to remain informed. By doing so, you will be better able to prepare your finances and your marketing strategy for future changes to government regulations.

Turning Lemons into Lemonade

I recently had an agent call me on the phone, and he was absolutely panicked about the prospect of Zillow and iBuyers "taking his business." First of all, I told him, it's not "your business" to take. You have to earn every deal; it's not a birthright. And in a free, capitalist marketplace, you have to wake up every morning and compete with others to earn the trust of the public and their business. So if you really view iBuyers as a threat to your business, then why not adopt the well-known mantra of, "If you can't beat them, join them?"

That's right—partner with some flippers/investors or even other iBuyer companies, and work with them to offer sellers the option to get an instant offer. Most sellers still prefer to work with an agent to get top dollar for their home, but this allows you to offer a service comparable to the leading iBuyer programs. This is a viable option for your business, and devoting your time to working on this program to offer sellers a full suite of options is time much better spent than just complaining and trying to organize a boycott of the thing you don't like. Not to mention, anti-competitive behavior like organizing boycotts of competing establishments is a potential legal violation of antitrust laws.

Cloud Agent Suite is one such service you can use to generate iBuyer offers for your clients.

The benefits of doing this are many, including giving your clients more options. But it also ensures that you as the agent stay involved in the transaction. Even if a seller decides to go the iBuyer route, wouldn't it be helpful if they had a real estate expert who could help them choose the best iBuyer offer? You may have to reduce the commission you charge, but it's still going to be more than the $0 you would have made if you just threw a hissy fit instead of adapting.

The most successful agents have mastered the art of adapting. Our world is in a constant state of change, and the real estate industry is no different, so don't ever rest on your laurels or you'll end up going the way of Blockbuster Video.

Once you adopt this mindset, it's amazing how zany the anti-Zillow warriors sound. You know who isn't screaming their head off about Zillow and iBuyers? Top producers. That's because they are too busy selling homes! Consider that.

8

How to Generate Business

The goal of all agents is to eventually earn all their business by referral. When you're just starting out as a new agent, you are mostly going to be getting your leads from prospecting methods like door-knocking or phone calls. You also begin incorporating marketing methods that are more sophisticated but still not ideal due to the associated cost.

Some Leads Are Better Than Others

Remember to prioritize your leads. Your top priority should always be people who are most likely to send you referrals, like past clients, friends, and family who have previously sent you a referral. The next priority should be your sphere of influence. These are past clients, friends, and family who could send you a referral but haven't done so yet. All other leads fall into the next categories.

Perfect the Art of Plate Spinning...Kinda

It's important not to be over-reliant on any one source of business leads. The more sources of leads the more stability you have in your business. You can think of this like spinning plates. Sure, the performer spinning one plate is impressive, but the performer spinning two plates it's even more so, and the performer spinning five plates, including one off the tip of their nose, is putting the other two people out of business! You want to have as many plates spinning as possible at the same time. The goal is to eventually build up to a largely referral-based business that you will continue to feed with your marketing and prospecting efforts.

There are many reasons why referral-based business is best. Referrals take less time and work on your part to close the transaction. Referred leads are typically going to be more trusting of you and more loyal more to you. Everyone hates flaky clients, and you'll encounter far fewer flakes when you're working largely by referral. Clients who are referred to you also tend to be amazing sources of new referrals. So if you do a great job, there is a good chance that you will pick up some new referrals from their family, friends, and coworkers.

Forget Me Not

So many agents spend countless dollars to acquire leads in the hopes that they will convert into a client. But then as soon as the client closes their transaction, the agent moves on to their next lead and completely forgets about their last client. This is a perfect recipe for your past clients choosing another agent to help them on their next transaction or referring another agent to a friend of theirs instead of you. You can easily remedy this by simply keeping in touch with your past clients. Set reminders for important dates like the anniversary of the purchase of their home and birthdays. Send little gifts quarterly or twice a year. How do you feel when you get a little unexpected gift in the mail? I bet it makes you feel good, no matter what kind of junk was sent. As they say, it's the thought that counts. With that in mind, make sure to surprise past clients with a small token of your appreciation for their continued business and referrals—not to mention a reminder who their favorite real estate agent is—wink, wink.

Trust me, if they're not hearing from you, they are definitely hearing from other agents, so your goal is to always be top of mind.

CRM = ABC's of Success

Having a reliable CRM system or customer relationship management system is one way that you can keep track of all of your clients, their personal details, when you last contacted them, and to set reminders to stay in touch. A CRM is the foundation for any successful real estate agent.

So now you're likely wondering, "What's the best CRM for real estate agents?" The answer, of course, is the one that you *use*.

Just do a simple internet search for "best real estate CRM" and you'll be met with an endless list of options. Some are simple and streamlined, some have all the bells and whistles. At the end of the day, you want the CRM that you will utilize. A CRM that you don't sign into every day is not a CRM worth having. So you're just going to have to dive in and try out the different options available before finding the right fit for you. If you find yourself not signing in for several days in a row, it might be a sign that your CRM isn't the best match for you. That's okay! There are hundreds of others out there just waiting to be your digital daily accountability partner.

Choosing Your Lead Generation Methods

When you are just starting out as an agent, your referral sources will be limited when compared to an experienced agent who has been doing this for years and has a pipeline of happy clients ready to send referrals. So you will have to work diligently at other lead generation methods in order to jump-start your business. Some popular lead generation options include sitting open houses, door-knocking, phone calling, marketing to expired and for-sale-by-owner listings, direct mail marketing, online advertising, and many others.

Similar to choosing the best CRM for you, the best lead generation method is the one that you actually do. Bonus points if it doesn't feel like having your teeth pulled.

Expired Listings

When you are prospecting expired listings, it is important to remember that your competition is likely to be fierce and the owner of the expired listing is probably getting calls non-stop by agents in your boat trying to get their business.

Why are expired listings such competitive prospecting sources? It's because you know that the property owner wants to sell their property—they already had it listed for sale. Your job is to find out why the property didn't sell and then to convince the owner why they should relist the property with you. Keep in mind that the biggest reason for an expired listing is that the property was overpriced. The seller is likely frustrated and they are just looking for someone who can sell their home. You must be prepared to communicate effectively with someone who is probably not in a great mood. You'll need to be able to effectively explain your marketing methods and your pricing strategy. Remember, most sales aren't made until the third or fourth phone call, so do not be discouraged when you are hung up on after making your first call. Stay consistent and call back a week later and continue calling back for about 45 days, every week or so.

FSBO - for Sale by Owner

FSBO's, a.k.a. for-sale-by-owner properties are similar to expired listings in that we know the property owner wants to sell. The only difference really is that this seller has decided to try to do it all on their own, without utilizing the services of a real estate agent. Oftentimes, sellers who go the FSBO route think that by forgoing the services of a real estate professional, they are saving money, but in reality, they lack the market knowledge, experience, and negotiating know-how that professionals possess, usually resulting in less money for the seller. Not to mention the increased legal liability from an inexperienced seller representing themself in a transaction. There's a saying about a person who is their own lawyer and how they have a fool for a client. I think the same can be said about trying to sell your own home without the help of a professional.

With all that in mind, for-sale-by-owner properties are excellent prospecting resources for you to go after. They tend to have less competition than expired listings, but like expired listings, you are going to need to be diligent in your contact attempts, and you're going to need to give the property owner a reason you want to return your phone call. Here's a dirty little secret: a lot of agents will fib to property owners and tell them that they have a buyer who is interested in the property; their hope is that once they get the listing, then a buyer will show up. But if you have to start your relationship with a client on a lie, then it's probably not going to be a great relationship in the long run. Instead, lead with honesty. Try to provide them something of value in return or an appointment. This can be something as simple as the standard disclosure forms in your area. This is certainly valuable to a property owner planning to sell their home by themself, and it also gives them an idea of just how significant the legal and disclosure requirements are when selling a home. So while the potential client will view the item as a nice gift, it also serves as a kind of Trojan Horse that gets you inside the home and inside the seller's brain. When they finally give up trying to sell the home by themself, you will be top of mind.

Where to Find FSBOs

So how do you find for-sale-by-owner properties? The easiest way is with subscription services that you can find with a simple internet search. This is really the best bet because maximizes your time and makes you more efficient. If you don't yet have the funds for a subscription service, you can always start by browsing your local classified ads or websites specifically for for-sale-by-owner listings.

Here are some tips to have the best chance of success when prospecting for-sale-by-owner properties:

Try as much as possible to be the first person who contacts the seller. Not only does the early bird get the worm; they also get the listing.

Don't lie. Be honest and upfront, and don't be a jerk. This should go without saying, but unfortunately, it needs to be said.

Impress them. I cannot overstate this enough. Show up prepared: bring a prelisting package, bring some of your marketing materials, bring your marketing plans, show local statistics, have graphs, provide a checklist of things that you will do in marketing the property, and offer a checklist of things that the seller should do to make sure that their home looks as good as possible for showings. This is your chance, so don't blow it.

Listen. Even though most for-sale-by-owner properties are listed that way in order to try and save money, you should not assume that that is the only or the primary reason why the property is listed without an agent. Maybe they had a really bad experience previously with a real estate agent, or maybe they are just independent-minded and wanted to give it a go on their own. It's important that you make sure to listen to the homeowner and pay attention to what they are saying when you speak with them. Listen out for clues as to why they decided to sell the home themself. The very best agents are the ones who can change up their presentation to address concerns that the seller brought up earlier in conversation.

Open Houses as a Source of New Business

Want to know a little secret? Most agents hold open houses in order to pick up buyer and seller leads. Thanks to the internet, open houses are rarely the source of the ultimate buyer of the property. Nowadays, buyers find the property online and then we'll either schedule a visit or tour the property at the next scheduled open house.

Now, even though many agents do use open houses as a lead-generation tool, they can still be really great for getting a home sold for top dollar. For example, in a seller's market, it can often be a good strategy to decline private showings in lieu of one- or two-weekend open houses, with small time windows, so instead of 12 p.m. to 4 p.m., maybe only do it from 12 p.m. to 2 p.m. By narrowing the available time of the open house and ensuring that all interested buyers are only able to see the property at the open house, you stand a good chance of generating a heated bidding war, where basically the various buyers touring the home get caught up in the buzz and excitement for the property and they kind of feed off each other's feeling of, "Wow, this house is cool *and* everyone wants it." So I absolutely do recommend open houses for actually selling houses when done correctly and for the right reason. Otherwise, open houses are really just a great way for you to meet buyers and sellers and try to turn them into clients.

Some Tips for Successfully Prospecting at Your Open House

- Depending on the size of the home, plan to arrive anywhere from 30 minutes to 90 minutes early to ensure everything is ready and the property is presentable; that means all lights on and all interior doors open.
- Have a sign-up sheet, whether it's on paper or with an iPad or other digital device (just be careful of theft; this may not be a reasonable option depending on your location). You will want to collect every visitor's name and contact information, not just for your own prospecting uses, but also to show the seller how successful you were and how hard you are

working to get the property sold.

- Have something to give away to visitors, such as a marketing brochure, a home buyer's guide, or even a little bottle of water with your information on it.
- Make sure you follow up. Preferably, follow up the same day, in order to get their immediate feedback and also to see if there is a potential chance to work with them.
- **Bonus**: Use the feedback you receive from the follow up and provided it to the seller as a way for them to hear some honest feedback from real buyers who toured the home.

Conclusion

Here's the thing: the very best agents are the ones who consistently start their day at the same time and who work various lead generation sources: from for-sale-by-owners, to expired listings, to open houses. The best agents use their time to generate new business. When you are just starting out in real estate, there is no other way to generate reliable business.

Bonus Prospecting Scripts

Here's a great prospecting script for general situations:

Hi, this is Alex Agent calling from ABC Real Estate. I do the majority of my business in your area and I don't think we've had a chance to meet yet, so I was just calling to see if you had any real estate means that I could help you with. Oh you don't? Okay, well I can see why you don't want to move—it's a great neighborhood that you live in. Have you ever wondered what your home could be worth in today's market? I don't mind if you're interested in selling or not. I don't mind stopping by to give you a home value estimate just so you know what your house is worth if you're ever thinking about selling.

Here's a great one for prospecting current renters:

Hi it's Alex Agent calling from ABC Real Estate. How are you? I was just calling today to see if you have ever considered moving out and owning your own home instead of renting? The reason why I'm calling is that we have some great properties perfect for new owners that are available right now. They're in really good condition, and the prices are great. In a lot of cases right now, many people are finding that their mortgage is actually lower than their rents. And the best part is that instead of paying a landlord every month, you're paying down property that you own. Would you be interested in going over the numbers sometime to see if owning makes sense for you?

Here's a great script that you can use to ask for referrals from past clients:

Hi it's Alex Agent calling from ABC Real Estate. How are you? It's so nice to hear your voice (make small talk). The reason I'm calling is to tell you that I'm always here to answer your real estate questions. Please don't ever hesitate to contact me. I hope you know how much I appreciate having you as a client, and if you know anyone who is considering buying or selling, I would love to be able to help them. Will it be okay with you if I sent you a few business cards that you could pass out to your friends? It would really mean the world to me, and you know I would take amazing care of them.

Here's one you can use for prospecting the new referral you got:

Hi this is Alex Agent calling from ABC Real Estate. How are you? I was actually talking to Sally Smithers yesterday, and she mentioned that you were considering looking for a new house. Well, I was Sally's real estate agent when she sold her last house, and she gave me your information. I would love to send you some info that you can read over. Would that be all right with you?

Here's a script you can use for expired listings:

Hi this is Alex Agent calling from ABC Real Estate I was calling today to see if your house at 321 Evergreen Terrace is still for sale. Oh, it's not? Well, are you still looking to sell? What if I had a buyer ready to go? Out of curiosity, why do you think your home didn't sell? Well, I would love to come by and take a look to see if your home might match the needs of one of my buyers or one of my colleagues' buyers. Can we do that this Thursday?

Here's an open house script you can use:

Hello, this is Alex Agent calling from ABC Real Estate. I was calling to thank you for coming to the open house that I hosted today at 555 Strawberry Lane. Would you mind if I asked you a few questions just to get some feedback that I can provide my home seller? Great, thank you. Did you like the house? How did you find out about the open house? Did you know that I have access to properties as soon as they get listed and you might not see those for hours or days later? Sometimes by that point, the home is already under contract with another buyer. Can I get some more information about what you're looking for in a home? That way I can send you listings as soon as they hit the market and you can be one of the first people to tour it.

9

Marketing Yourself for Success

Experienced, established real estate agents often receive a considerable amount of their business from referrals and from repeat clients. As a new real estate agent, you must drive leads to you through an effective marketing campaign. Your primary goal through marketing is to connect with buyers and sellers at a point when they need your services. However, reaching out to those who are not currently ready to buy or sell is important. This can make them more familiar with your name and image. When they are ready to move forward, they may be more likely to connect with you.

What does it take to develop and execute an effective marketing campaign? Because you are developing your campaign from scratch, you will need to spend a considerable amount of time and energy developing your message and refining your approach. Once you find what works, however, you can put some aspects of your marketing efforts on autopilot.

Develop Your Message

Your marketing message needs to tell potential clients who you are, what value you will bring to their transaction, and what sets you apart from other professionals who are also vying for their attention. Essentially, why should they contact you? As you craft your message, a great starting point is to review marketing from other established, successful real estate agents in your area. While this will give you an idea of what can work, your message must be unique and personalized specifically to you.

You may have a general message for both buyers and sellers, but you may also create unique value propositions. For example, being native to the community is a value proposition for marketing to both buyers and sellers. Working with a broker that has a great track record of selling homes quickly is a value proposition for seller-focused marketing.

While your marketing message should be short and sweet, it also should be filled with detail. For example, do you have special services that not all agents offer? Concisely highlight what makes you different and better.

As a sales professional, the effectiveness of your marketing message can also make a statement about how strong your professional skills are. If your message selling yourself jumps out at a buyer or seller, that individual may believe that you have what it takes to help with their purchase or sale transaction.

Portions of your marketing message may change minimally in the years ahead. Messaging surrounding your brand identity, for example, is not likely to change year-to-year. Other portions may be adjusted based on the season, market conditions, and more. For example, your message during a buyer's market will be different from your message during a seller's market.

Create a Website

You should not rely solely on the small online presence that your broker has given you on the company's website. While you work under a broker, you are focusing on a specific niche, and you have unique value propositions that you want to highlight. More than that, you want to stand out from others who work under your broker. After all, those real estate agents are your competition. Investing in the creation of a professional website is essential.

A well-designed website showcases your skills and services, and it positions you as a true professional. More than that, effectively integrating search engine optimization strategies into the website can turn your website into a lead generation tool. Ensure that your website has a lead capture feature on it and multiple action items.

In addition to these benefits, your website encourages interaction, and it gives visitors a reason to come back. Perhaps that reason is to check out the newest listings to hit the market or to read your latest blog post. Your website can also direct traffic elsewhere, such as through email and social media sharing buttons.

Keep in mind that many people use smartphones and other mobile devices to browse the internet. You will undoubtedly spend a lot of time and energy driving traffic to your website, so the last thing that you want is for that traffic to bounce off because of poor formatting. Internet users will not spend time exploring your website if they are frustrated with a poor linking strategy, slow load times, and bad flow. Ensure that your website is properly formatted for optimized view across all devices.

Use Social Media

Social media platforms give you a direct and cost-effective way to reach out to established and new leads. Popular platforms that real estate agents use regularly are Facebook, Twitter, Instagram, and LinkedIn. Be aware that how you utilize these platforms should vary. For example, Instagram is an image-based platform that may be ideal for showing off new listings. Twitter can be used in the same way, but it can also be used to advertise new blog posts and to stay in touch with clients in other ways. Each platform has its strengths that you can tap into for optimal results.

To maximize the effectiveness of social media platforms for marketing purposes, you need to post content regularly. However, the content should be meaningful rather than spammy. Posting spam is a good way to lose followers and to ruin the image that you are spending time developing. Consider creating a social media marketing calendar so that posts are published in a timely manner and so that the content is prepared meaningfully.

Each time you create a post, you should ask your followers to take action. For example, ask them to share a listing with their own followers, to share thoughts, or to connect with you for more information. Remember that social media is meant to be social. This means that you should check your accounts regularly and reply promptly to your followers. By doing so, you can establish rapport with individuals you may not have had the opportunity to do so with otherwise.

Publish a Blog

Your website is the perfect outlet for publishing a blog. A well-written blog post can help to showcase your expertise. For example, it may highlight staging tips, share current market data, or talk about the best time to buy or sell a home. Some content may be evergreen, and other content may be specific for current market conditions. All content, however, will give your website's visitors as well as your followers a reason to spend more time on your website.

Some people will find your blog posts organically, such as through a direct internet search. Perhaps they discovered your posts because one of your followers shared it. These are new leads that have been directly generated by blog posts, so ensure that you capture those leads. To do so, your blog posts should each have a lead capture form.

Search engine optimization essentially means that your website is structured so that search engines can more easily identify its content and purpose and so that they will rank the website higher for relevant searches. SEO has become incredibly complex over the years. Everything from your website's structure to page load times, backlinks, and more will play a role in rankings. However, choosing the right combination of keywords to target and incorporating them into your content naturally continues to be essential for great results. More than that, the age of your content plays a role in search engine results.

Your blog posts give you a chance to target keywords that your website may have otherwise not ranked well for. It also enables you to maintain fresh content and even to build opportunities for backlinks. The power of blog posts is considerable. If you do not have the skill or time to write the posts yourself, there are a variety of online platforms that you can use to get in touch with freelance writers.

Build Your Database

There are various ways to find names and contact information for potential buyers and sellers, such as by purchasing lists and scouring property tax records. Generally, efforts to connect with individuals through these ways are considered to be spam because those individuals did not ask to be on a mailing or emailing list. While it is a slower method, you may discover that you will see a much better response when you build your own database by capturing leads. There are a few different methods that enable you to do so.

For example, on each of your blog post pages and on various other pages on the website, you can create lead capture forms. You may drive visitors to your website through flyers on front yard signs, organically through SEO, by paying for advertising, and more. When the visitors arrive at your website, the lead capture form enables you to convert a visitor into a lead. Likewise, you can use chatbots on your website, on Facebook, and in other areas to capture leads.

If you use lead generation forms, ask for more information than a name, a phone number, and an email address. By getting details about whether they are a buyer or seller, when they are planning to act, and more, you can customize the marketing material that you send to them.

Create a Call-to-Action Statement

You can spend a lot of time, energy, and money creating an amazing marketing campaign, and you understandably want to see positive results. For each unique marketing message that you put out, ask yourself what you want to accomplish. Do you want someone to follow you on Facebook, to download an ebook, to fill out a lead generation form, or to take another action?

A call-to-action statement asks or invites someone to take a specific action. Some people believe that a call-to-action statement is too bossy or obvious, but the reality is that these statements work. In fact, they work so well that you may consider embedding multiple statements throughout a single page on your website.

An effective call-to-action statement does more than ask someone to take action; it tells them how they will benefit by doing so. These statements should be concise and direct. Avoid using if-then statements. Instead, use command verb tenses. An example of an effective call-to-action statement would be, "Sign up today to learn more about selling your home in today's hot market."

Offer Value Through a Lead Magnet

People love to receive free items that they perceive as valuable. When you offer free items of value, you are creating a lead magnet. For example, you may create a free seller's how-to guide, tips to follow before buying your first home, a hot list of homes currently for sale, and other content. To receive this free information, a visitor simply needs to fill out the lead generation form and sign up. Essentially, you are creating a powerful reason for someone to sign up and to join your lead database.

Initially, your lead database will be small, and you may see very little activity from it. However, as it continues to grow, you will see the powerful impact that it will have on your business. Growing a database can take a significant amount of time and effort. You may only add a few new leads to it across some months. Other months, you may add more than 100 new entries to the database. Stay focused, and you will gradually see the results that you want.

Use Direct Marketing Methods Strategically

Direct marketing is any type of marketing that directly reaches the intended audience. For example, mailed promotional materials will arrive in a person's mailbox. You can feel confident that your audience will hold your material in their hands. At that point, they must decide whether to open and read the material. While there is no guarantee that the message will be read, you are assured that the material will be received. A great tip here is to send postcards rather than material in an envelope. This makes your message immediately visible when the postcard is in the audience's hands. No additional steps are required, so your message is more likely to be viewed.

There are a variety of direct marketing methods, and the options that are most commonly used by real estate agents to attract new leads are direct mail and door-to-door flyers. Often, a real estate agent will target one specific neighborhood using these methods. By refining the target audience in this way, you can focus your message so that it is relevant to their needs. An alternative is to focus on an apartment complex by offering buyer's services and market information that is relevant to buyers.

Direct mail also works well when marketing to established leads. Using your database of leads, you can utilize email and text messaging to send direct, focused messages to those who have opted in to receive messages from you. For example, a quick text message stating facts about a recent sale in the community and an open question regarding if they are thinking about selling soon could work well.

Consider Paid Online Advertising

There are costs associated with some of the marketing methods discussed up to this point, such as printing and distribution costs for mailers and flyers. You can also pay for online advertising to attract leads.

For example, an online banner ad could have minimal cost and may yield great results if it is properly placed. A banner ad placed on a local mortgage broker's website or any websites with content related to first-time homebuyers, selling homes, downsizing, upgrading, and more could work well. Paid online advertising should be geographically specific. When you choose the keywords that you want to target, you should choose those related to your metropolitan area, suburbs you focus on, and any other geographic references that are relevant to your target audience.

In addition to pay-per-click advertising campaigns, such as through Google, you can run ads on social media platforms. Facebook allows you to pay for ads that can be targeted to a specific target audience. This could be an effective way to encourage your target audience to follow you on social media or to visit your website. One type of ad involves creating a post for a blog you recently published and paying to promote your post. By doing so, your ad may appear in your target audience's feeds even if they are not an active follower.

Paid online advertising can seem too expensive when you are just starting out. After all, you may be stressed about spending money before you have even closed one or two transactions. You have bills to pay, and you are unsure when money will start flowing in. The good thing about paid online advertising are that it can be finely focused and you can set a budget. For example, you can cap Facebook ads at a few dollars per day, and you can put a top cap of less than $100 on the total campaign.

Ask for Referrals and Repeat Business

Many established real estate agents obtain the bulk of their business from referrals and repeat clients. This could be a long-term goal for you, and you can begin working toward that goal today. Those who choose to do business with you again and who send their friends and family members your way are individuals who are very pleased with their overall experience and with the results that you delivered. This means that generating business in this fashion requires you to provide a consistently excellent experience from the first conversation.

As you nurture leads and serve clients, focus on building relationships that can last for years rather than solely working toward a paycheck. Respond to inquiries promptly and follow through on what you say you will do. Work on professional development, such as refining your negotiation and communication skills. Listen, be friendly, and approach the service that you provide from the perspective of helping that client achieve his or her unique goals.

Providing great service throughout the transaction is the cornerstone of building referrals and repeat business, but this is not enough. Take time at the end of a successful transaction to thank a client for the opportunity to serve him or her. Ask the client to keep you in mind for referrals and for future real estate needs. Periodically, as you continue to keep in touch with your leads, ensure that a small amount of space in your message is dedicated specifically to referrals.

Pull It All Together

While some real estate agents will focus on one or two specific marketing opportunities that have been discussed here, the best results are enjoyed when a well-rounded campaign with a strong message is prepared and executed. Take time today to prepare a marketing budget. As you start out, your budget may be solely allocated toward methods that generate new leads, but your allocation will adjust slightly over time as you get more leads in your database.

A new campaign should include preparing a website and setting up social media accounts. With a limited budget available, consider writing blog posts and promoting them through social media platforms. If you have more funds available from day one, a guerilla marketing campaign with door-to-door flyer delivery or a direct-mail campaign may help you to generate a few initial leads as well.

You may be enticed to simply rush through your marketing efforts in the hope of getting a client immediately. While that is a goal, it is best to prepare a full campaign using a calendar. Some of your marketing efforts will reach the same people multiple times. As people get more familiar with your name through well-timed touches, they may be more likely to connect with you when they need your services down the road. Create a monthly campaign that is aligned with your budget and that is seasonally appropriate. For example, a blog post in November could talk about selling a home during the holidays.

Respond to Inquiries Promptly

Clients are the lifeblood of your real estate career, so they should receive your full attention when they reach out to you. Many people contact a real estate agent for the first time when they are toying with the idea of selling or buying a home. They want information promptly, and they can lose interest in working with you quickly. In addition, they can also reach out to other real estate agents who may be easier to get in touch with if you wait too long to respond to an inquiry.

You understandably want to reap the maximum return from your marketing efforts, and you can see that responding promptly is a critical component to that. When you do connect with a lead, ask for permission to send them information and to stay in touch until they are ready to move forward. Offer sellers the opportunity to receive a free comparative market analysis, and offer to connect buyers with a mortgage lender for their prequalification. This is your chance to get the ball rolling. At the same time, you can offer guidance through the process while also showing off your expertise. By doing so, you are continuing to market yourself.

Fine-Tune and Automate Your Campaign

You will undoubtedly discover that some of your marketing efforts are far more effective than others. In some cases, if your marketing is not effective, you should refine your message so that it appeals to your target audience. Your message could also be adjusted so that it is aligned with market conditions and the season. In other cases, the marketing method itself may not be a cost-effective solution for reaching your specific target audience. Make strategic adjustments to your campaigns so that you can improve results over time.

Your initial goal is to build a database of leads and secure clients. Your long-term goal is to establish a stream of referrals and repeat clients. Keep these goals in mind as you fine-tune your marketing efforts so that those efforts can be properly focused.

Marketing will inevitably consume a sizable portion of your time because of its importance, but your goal is to spend the majority of your time nurturing leads and serving clients. With this in mind, look for ways to automate your campaign when possible.

For example, you can automate the dispatch of your seller's how-to guide or current market data after a potential client opts in to receive your marketing material. You can also schedule email marketing and text message marketing so that a small, manageable batch of contacts is touched daily. This is often better than sending out thousands of emails in one day and being overwhelmed with the response.

When marketing is carefully planned and properly executed, it can provide you with a steadily growing stream of leads. Because of the importance of marketing to real estate agents, look for ways to improve your knowledge in this area as part of your ongoing professional development.

10

Working with Sellers

As a real estate agent, you need to develop a standard business model that sets you up for optimized success. Generally, you can choose to serve buyers, sellers, or both. Many real estate agents love spending time touring homes with their clients and assisting in the selection of their dream home. However, when your goal is to optimize profitability, listing homes is clearly advantageous. Whether you focus solely on serving sellers or your services extend to both buyers and sellers, seller services should be included in your business model to a significant degree.

Listings Are Life

In order to appreciate the true value that lies in serving sellers, a deeper look at the services provided by a buyer's agent and a seller's agent is in order. Your time is limited as a real estate agent, so your profitability directly hinges on your ability to be as efficient as possible. Of course, this efficiency should not be at the expense of providing your clients with exceptional service and meeting your obligations to them.

A buyer's agent is tasked with helping a client locate a home that is ideal for his or her expectations, needs, and budget. While some buyers are relatively easy to work with, many are concerned about making an offer on the wrong home. As a result, they often continue searching for a home before circling back to one that they previously toured. You can realistically spend many long hours spread across days or weeks trying to help that client find the right home. In the event that the client decides to hold off on buying a home, this represents lost time to you.

As a seller's agent, on the other hand, your upfront work generally consists of the listing presentation and all preliminary work associated with that. As is the case with the preliminary work that you would do with a client as a buyer's agent, there is no guarantee that a listing presentation will turn into a listing. However, the amount of time and energy spent working on a listing presentation and actually making your pitch are often dramatically less than what it takes to find the perfect home for a buyer.

The appeal of representing sellers extends to the contract negotiation phase. The buyer's agent is responsible for preparing and presenting an offer. In the event that multiple offers have been made, the seller's agent has the advantage. This is because the seller could accept any of the offers available without necessarily increasing the workload of the seller's agent. On the other hand, if the buyer's offer is not accepted in a multiple-offer situation, the buyer's agent may need to start taking the buyer on home tours again.

That being said, the buyer's agent and the seller's agent in a typical transaction split the commission evenly. If you want to optimize efficiency and profitability, serving sellers is clearly advantageous. However, if you enjoy serving buyers as well, there is room to profit from serving the needs of buyers and sellers alike.

How Do You Wow Sellers?

Given the tremendous benefits that come from representing a seller, you understandably want to do your part to win more listings. What does it take to wow a seller? It starts with your approach. Generally, a seller will contact you because of your marketing efforts or from a referral. A prelisting report is an excellent marketing tool because it serves as an informative resource for the potential client. This tool should provide general market information as well as details about your experience and success. Stats as well as short snippets that outline details of a recent transaction work well.

When a potential client contacts you, do not skimp on the important matter of touring the home. This gives you the chance to get to know the client and to identify any strengths and weaknesses that affect the value and the appeal of the home to potential buyers. You will then follow up on that initial meeting with the client for a professional listing presentation.

The presentation should appeal to the seller's hot buttons that you identified during the first meeting. At the same time, it should sell the services that you provide that differentiate you from other real estate agents. Specifically, include a professional marketing plan that outlines all of the channels that you plan to use. This includes various listing sites, open houses, social media, and more. Your services may include providing resources for prelisting preparations and staging assistance. You may also pay for professional photos and videos, 3D tours, drone videos, and other benefits out of your fees as a service to your clients.

The listing presentation should abide by the "Rule of 3's for Recommendations." Provide three recommendations to potential clients that show suggested list prices based on different pricing strategies. In addition to putting the seller in the driver's seat, this rule reduces your exposure to liability.

Wow Sellers by Marketing Like Crazy!

While some houses seemingly sell themselves, most properties must be extensively marketed. After all, through marketing, potential buyers and their agents learn about your listing and about its key selling points. Adding a listing to the MLS is essential, but this is only the tip of the iceberg for developing an effective marketing campaign.

Print, direct, and online advertising all play key roles in a well-rounded campaign. Print media encompasses magazines and newspapers. In your listing presentation, be specific about which publications you intend to run ads in. Another idea is to pitch a home to a large newspaper. When successful, large publications may run a feature article about the home to maximize exposure.

Direct marketing may include a guerilla marketing campaign where you disperse flyers throughout a neighborhood or community. This also includes direct mailers, such as postcards and other materials. Your listing presentation should include specific details regarding the number of direct materials that will be circulated.

Online advertising includes the MLS listing, and it also encompasses other popular listing sites, such as Zillow and Redfin. Social media marketing, blog posts, and other methods may also be used.

Stay in Touch

The initial effort that a buyer's agent makes to serve clients is obvious. After all, a buyer's agent actively shows homes to his or her client until a suitable property is located. In comparison, most of the upfront work that a seller's agent does to attract a buyer is done behind the scenes. From the seller's perspective, it can appear as though you are doing little to earn your commission if you are not actively communicating with the client. This is particularly true if many showings have not been scheduled.

It's fun to work in a field where you are called an agent, but no matter how much it makes you think of spies, being an actual "secret agent" can work against and may ultimately cause you to lose a listing. Instead of being a secret agent, you want to be the well-know agent. A smart idea is to provide your clients with weekly updates. Include important details like previous and active marketing efforts. For efforts that you have stats on, provide those stats in your update. For example, MLS, Zillow, and Redfin provide rankings for you to disclose to your client. You can also outline website hits, completed home tours, and scheduled tours. Then, go a step further to outline how the property will be marketed over the course of the next week. By staying in touch with your client, you are actively highlighting the hard work that you are doing. You are also showing off your marketing expertise, and this can ultimately lead to future referrals from satisfied clients.

Honesty Is the Best Policy

Despite a listing agent's best efforts to market a home, there are several factors that can work against you. Regardless of how impressive the house is, it will be hard to sell if it is overpriced. Some sellers have an unreasonable view of their home's appeal, and others do not understand how market fluctuations impact price. As a result, they may insist that their home is listed for a specific dollar amount that is far higher than what the market can support. Furthermore, they may be unwilling to negotiate when a more reasonable offer is presented by an interested party.

You may also be challenged to sell a home that is ugly even if it is priced well. An ugly home may be one with outdated design elements or a poor layout. It could also have updated or modern materials that are not appealing to most buyers. Homes that appeal to a limited number of potential buyers may take much longer to sell.

Some homes stay on the market much longer than necessary because the seller is stubborn or unreasonable. For example, if the carpet is worn out, it is reasonable for an interested buyer to ask for a carpet allowance, for the carpet to be replaced before closing, or for the sales price to be adjusted to account for the cost of new carpet. When a seller is not willing to negotiate reasonably, the interested buyers that you attract through your marketing efforts may walk away.

As a seller's agent, your job is to successfully facilitate the sale. This means that you must approach situations like these directly. Some real estate agents do not want to risk angering a client and losing a listing. However, these and other similar situations directly thwart your ability to facilitate the sale of the property. Honesty is always the best policy in such situations. Your tactful approach to delivering feedback is ultimately essential in your ability to do your job properly.

The Pros and Cons of Popular Pricing Strategies

Savvy listing agents have deep knowledge of popular pricing strategies, and they know when and how to incorporate these strategies into their listing presentations. In some cases, these popular strategies can be blended together to benefit the client. What are the more popular pricing strategies?

Pricing Based on Comparable Sales Analysis

The bread and butter of a listing presentation is a comparable sales analysis. This approach compares the client's property to several similar properties in the vicinity that have sold recently. Because no two houses are the same, the real estate agent can take some price-adjustment liberties based on factors like recent upgrades, bonus features, and other factors.

The comparable sales analysis approach does not take into account many of the factors that the seller may perceive as adding value to the home. Many people who have poured their heart, soul, and personal funds into home improvements may not view the actual value of these investments in a manner that aligns with the market. This can make the comparable sales analysis valuation difficult to sell to some homeowners. However, this reasonable approach may reduce the chance of an interested buyer attempting major negotiations or making a lowball offer.

Pricing Adjustments Based on Online Visibility

According to the National Association of Realtors, approximately 44 percent of buyers begin their search for a new home online. Popular online real estate search platforms generally enable searches within a specific price range. For example, a buyer may search for homes priced between $300,000 and $325,000. Using this pricing strategy, rounding up to the highest threshold in that range will ensure that the listing is returned in search results for suitable buyers. At the same time, it can reduce the risk of leaving money on the table unnecessarily.

While this strategy may increase visibility and initial interest, it does not guarantee that the seller will receive higher offers. Ultimately, offers may be aligned with a comparable sales analysis strategy. In the event that the list price is substantially higher than what the market can support, some buyers who may otherwise be interested in the home may never make an offer because they perceive it as being overpriced.

Pricing Adjustments Based on the Season

Generally, there is a substantial uptick in listings as well as sales in the spring and summer months. In this type of environment, pricing the home to stand out is essential. As the end of summer approaches, pricing the home slightly higher may be reasonable. This is because many buyers are interested in finalizing their purchase and moving in before the beginning of the new school year. However, if the property is a small condo or townhouse in an area that is not popular with families, this may not be a factor.

In the fall and winter months, the number of listings and the number of buyers generally decrease. This means that the seller's home has less competition. In the event that it has unique and desired attributes, it may be reasonable to price the home slightly higher. If a seller has a tight timeline, however, pricing the home below market value in the fall and winter months may be necessary.

Pricing Set Below Market to Attract Attention Quickly

Regardless of the season, pricing a home below market value is a surefire way to attract attention initially. With this pricing strategy, the home may be larger and have greater appeal than other similar homes within the same price range in the vicinity. As a result, the home may be toured more heavily. In addition to potentially getting a fast offer, this strategy may result in the home receiving multiple offers. When this happens, a bidding war may drive the price up.

On the other hand, when a home is priced well below market value and remains on the market for a long period of time, buyers may assume that something is wrong with the home or that the seller is difficult to work with. Because of this, a home may receive less interest than it otherwise would if it does not sell quickly.

Pricing Set to Optimize Return

Some sellers insist on trying to optimize their return by asking for a price that is far above what the market can support. With this strategy, the seller is initially pleased with the listing agent's efforts and is hopeful about realizing a great return when the home sells. In reality, this strategy often results in very few home tours. The listing may generate minimal offers below the asking price or no offers at all. Eventually, the seller will grow frustrated. Some sellers may blame the lack of interest in the home on the real estate agent's poor marketing strategy.

If your client insists on using this pricing strategy, you must set realistic expectations upfront. Ensure that the client understands that this strategy could result in minimal response and potentially lower offers. Talk to the client about their comfort level for reducing the price if it has not sold within a certain number of days and about other approaches that may work well given the client's circumstances.

When to Say No to a Seller

Turning down the opportunity to list a home may seem like the last thing that you want to do, but there are instances when it must be done. For example, if any aspect of the listing or transaction would be illegal, you should walk away immediately. A Fair Housing violation, for another example, would occur if the seller refuses to sell his or her house to individuals based on their race, religion, origin, or other similar factors. This is only one of many instances when a client's demands may put you at risk of losing your real estate license and facing legal issues.

Another reason to walk away from a client is when he or she will not take your recommendations regarding pricing. When a client has unrealistic expectations regarding the price of their home, how quickly it could sell, and other aspects of the transaction, your first step is to counsel them by presenting facts and recommendations. If the client's unreasonable expectations persist, there is a possibility that you may never be able to sell the home or make the client happy. This is a recipe for considerable stress, an unhappy client who potentially can impact your professional reputation, and lost time and energy.

11

Working with Buyers

Helping your clients locate the perfect home and guiding them through the entire purchase process are infinitely rewarding for real estate agents. However, as a buyer's agent, you will also be faced with extensive challenges that affect everything from client satisfaction to your bottom line as an independent contractor.

As a buyer's agent, your responsibilities extend far beyond simply assisting with the home search. Establishing reasonable expectations, facilitating negotiations, and helping clients pay a fair amount for their home are also some of the more important duties of a buyer's real estate agent.

Your success as a buyer's agent is directly tied to your ability to provide the highest level of service to existing clients. Satisfied clients can result in referrals, and referrals are a vital source of new leads for real estate agents. With this in mind, what does it take to be a successful buyer's agent?

Where to Find Quality Leads

Before you can deliver amazing service to your valued clients, you must find quality leads and convert those into clients. As your client base expands, you may enjoy an increasing number of high-quality leads from referrals. Initially, however, most or all of your leads may directly be tied to your lead-generation efforts.

Through your brokerage firm, you may be able to pick up a phone-duty shift. Generally, all of the leads that you secure on a phone-duty shift are yours to work. However, you should carefully review your broker's policy related to these leads before spending your limited time answering phones.

Until you have a few listings of your own, you can also ask established real estate agents in your firm if you can host open houses for their listings. Many potential buyers who stop by to tour an open home will continue looking for the right house for their needs and budget. At an open house, you can directly meet with these individuals. This face-to-face meeting creates the opportunity to connect personally with potential clients. In many cases, you can secure contact information to follow up with the leads after you are done manning the open house. You could even lock in a dedicated appointment to show homes to some of these individuals in the near future while you are hosting the open house.

Another excellent source of new leads for a buyer's agent is renters. The primary obstacle when marketing to renters is differentiating tenants from property owners. Apartment buildings are filled with tenants who may be potential buyers, but you should choose the apartment complexes that you target with care. Consider researching the tenant requirements that different apartment complexes have with regards to credit scores, income, and other factors. These requirements can give you a fair idea about what communities may have tenants who are more likely to be in a position to become first-time homebuyers in the near future.

You can also generate leads by hosting buyer seminars. First-time buyer seminars, for example, may attract qualified individuals who rent apartments, condos, townhouses, and homes throughout the area. An alternative is to host separate seminars for current homeowners in the area who are ready to upgrade or downsize. Each of these groups will have unique concerns, so delivering separate presentations can be effective. In these presentations, find strategic ways to position yourself as a helpful expert while also providing attendees with truly valuable information.

Keep in mind that there are numerous other real estate agents in your local area that are vying for the attention of buyers. You must get your name out there in order to be considered by buyers, but this is not enough. You also need to actively connect with these individuals while demonstrating why you are the right agent to help them with their purchase.

What are some other ways for you to get your name in front of potential buyers? Maximize your reach on social media platforms. Build your list of followers on Twitter, Facebook, and other platforms. Then, publish helpful information that your followers may be likely to share with their own followers. A smart idea is to create regular blog posts with content that is specifically targeted at buyers in your area.

You can also blanket the area with a door-to-door flyer campaign or a direct-mail campaign. Generally, many of these pieces will find their way into the trash, but you can get a decent response rate with a solid marketing message.

How to Convince Buyers to Work with You

There is no single lead conversion strategy that works well with all potential clients. Generally, both first-time and experienced buyers want to find a trustworthy and responsive real estate agent. They expect their real estate agent to provide extensive expertise while helping them to achieve their goals. At the same time, many potential clients want to find an individual they have a good rapport with.

As important as it is for you to convert leads into clients, you also want to be discerning about who you work with. Your time and energy as a real estate agent are in limited supply, so it makes financial sense to identify potential clients you are likely to work well with and whose needs you can realistically meet. With this in mind, you should actively vet clients while they are vetting you.

Across all of your marketing material and when you are meeting with potential clients initially, always be yourself. At the same time, convey a sense of professionalism and expertise. Find ways to highlight your strengths. Finding the right clients to work for requires you to get to know their expectations and needs. Ask open-ended questions to determine if your strengths and skills are well-suited for that specific individual's needs. You can use the knowledge that you gain from asking these questions to demonstrate to the client why you are the best real estate agent for the job.

In most cases, a lead will not immediately be converted into a client. Instead, you likely will need to nurture the lead by remaining in touch with the individual over the course of days, weeks, or even months. Throughout this period of time, always remain professional and helpful. Use each touch as an opportunity to build rapport and to deliver personalized service. Remember to always follow through on what you say you are going to do. For example, if you tell a potential client that you will send over market stats later that day, ensure that you do so.

The Importance of Mortgage Preapprovals

Potential buyers who will use financing to pay for their purchase should obtain a mortgage preapproval from a reputable lender before seriously searching for a new home. There are several good reasons for this. From your perspective as a real estate agent, you only want to spend your time actively working for individuals who have the ability to complete a purchase transaction. For most buyers, this means getting approved for a home loan.

A mortgage preapproval gives you and the buyer insight on the price range of homes that you should be looking at. When you start out looking at homes that are priced outside of the buyer's range, unrealistic expectations may be established. Once established, these expectations may make it difficult for the buyer to find an appealing home in his or her price range. As a result, you could spend far more time presenting different properties to the client than you otherwise would need to. In this way, a preapproval enables you to more efficiently and successfully serve the client.

In addition to establishing a comfortable price range for the buyer, the preapproval process may identify specific issues that must be addressed before or during the process. For example, the client may need to file last year's tax return before he or she can qualify. If the client is applying for a VA loan, you and the client may need to only look at properties in good condition to meet VA loan requirements.

Some real estate agents will not actively serve new clients until after they have a preapproval. The unfortunate reality is that some people will start touring homes well before they are serious about buying a home in the near future. These individuals can drain your time and energy, and you may never receive compensation for your efforts. If you are approached by a potential buyer who is not yet pre-approved, you can use this opportunity to demonstrate your expertise upfront. For example, you can recommend several mortgage brokers to the client. At the same time, you can explain the importance of a preapproval. Those potential clients who are serious about moving forward with a purchase will quickly be back in touch with you when they have a mortgage preapproval letter in their hand.

Keep in mind that a mortgage preapproval letter is also a sales tool. You can attach the preapproval letter to an offer. This letter serves as a sign of the buyer's solid interest as well as proof of the buyer's ability to buy the home from a financial perspective. In a situation involving multiple offers, a mortgage preapproval letter may be vital. Also, some real estate agents will advise sellers not to accept an offer until after the buyer has been preapproved.

With all of these factors in mind, advising clients to get preapproved for a home mortgage early in the process is often beneficial. Consider establishing relationships with reputable mortgage brokers or lending representatives who you can refer your new clients to.

Helping Clients Narrow Down the Search

Finding qualified and eager clients to work with is only part of your challenge as a buyer's real estate agent. Your next challenge lies in helping each specific client identify a home that meets their unique needs and that is priced within a comfortable range. Many new clients will come to you with a list of homes that they found through an online search or by driving through neighborhoods. While you could start serving your clients by taking them to the houses they found, you will do them a true service by helping them to narrow down the scope of their search upfront.

The mortgage preapproval letter will give you a solid idea about the maximum price range that a client can look at, but many clients may feel more comfortable looking at more affordable homes. Speak candidly with your clients about their budget so that you can narrow down the options to homes that are most likely to be a great fit for them.

Whether you meet with a client initially over the phone or online, use the opportunity to determine what must-have features the client needs. In many cases, must-have features will cover square footage, the number of bedrooms and bathrooms, and specific amenities. For example, a home with hard flooring surfaces may be a firm requirement for a client with asthma. A client who works from home may need a separate bedroom or another private area in addition to the family's bedrooms and living spaces. A laundry room, the size of the garage, and even a fenced yard may also be nonnegotiable in many cases.

Buyers also may have mild to strong preferences. While these are negotiable, your client may be more inclined to make an offer if the home has at least a few of their preferred features or traits. Some of these may include extras like a pool, a hot tub, a fireplace, a finished basement, a large pantry, and more. Keep in mind that features that may be preferred for some clients may be essential for others. These same features may be unappealing to other clients. As you interview your clients, pay attention to the reasoning behind their needs and wants. Consider taking detailed notes and referring back to these notes so that you consistently provide a high level of personalized service to each client.

The Importance of Creativity and Flexibility

Through your efforts interviewing a client, you know what the client is looking for and why. This enables you to think outside the box and to look for creative solutions that the client has not yet considered. For example, if a client is focused on living in an area of town that may not be affordable, finding a home with a small rental space over the garage that is producing monthly income could be a solution.

Many clients will state that they have hard limits on a home's minimum square footage, its distance from work, and other factors. However, stretching beyond these limits slightly could reveal the ideal home for the client. For example, a client may say that he or she does not want to commute more than 15 minutes to work, but a beautiful home that is located 18 minutes from the workplace may meet all of the client's needs, wants, and budget requirements.

As you search for homes that may interest your client, you must know when to push the envelope and how far to push it. When you present the client with a listing that is slightly outside of his or her criteria, ensure that you explain why you are presenting the option. If you fail to deliver reasoning, the client may assume that you simply do not understand his or her needs and wants. This can ultimately lead to the loss of the client.

Establish Proper Expectations

Market conditions impact buyers and sellers in different ways, and both types of clients must be educated on these potential impacts. In a buyer's market, homes often remain on the market for a longer period of time, and there are fewer other buyers to compete with. A buyer's market often enables a buyer to feel comfortable shopping around and taking a few days to think things over before making an offer.

In a seller's market, on the other hand, fewer homes are on the market. In addition, there may be more buyers shopping for a new home. Under these conditions, a buyer should be ready to make an offer as soon as a suitable home is located. A home can be snatched up by another buyer if the client takes too long weighing the possibilities.

As a buyer's real estate agent, you must consistently remain informed about current market conditions in your area. Whether the average time that a listing is on the market is 14 days, 70 days, or somewhere in the middle, you must educate your client about how current market conditions will impact the process.

Assist Clients with Structuring Their Offer

Many people assume that the asking price for a home is its property value. In reality, many factors could be influencing the seller's list price. For example, the seller may need to pay off a high mortgage balance and cover closing costs, and the list price may be set higher than market value to meet the seller's goals. On the other hand, a seller may need to sell a home quickly and may be offering the property at a lower price as a result.

Your clients are depending on you to help them get a great deal on the home that they are interested in. It is your job as a buyer's real estate agent to compare comps and to give your clients a reasonable valuation based on recent home sales in the area.

Ensure that your clients understand the role that the property's appraised value will play in the financing process. A seller may list a home above market price, and a buyer may be willing to pay that price. However, the appraiser may arrive at a lower home value based on market data. Mortgage lenders generally will base their loan amount on the lesser of the sales price or the appraised value. In a situation like this, the approved loan amount may be less than the buyer was expecting. If the buyer has not financially prepared for this possibility, he or she may not realistically be able to follow through on the purchase.

A similar situation may arise in a seller's market when multiple buyers are bidding on a home. A buyer may need to bid higher than the home's actual value in order to get the seller's attention. Regardless of the reason why the seller and buyer have come to an agreement on sales price, the property value as determined by the appraiser will impact the transaction. You must review market comps so that you can provide your client with proper guidance when structuring their offer.

Safety Tips for Showing Properties

Regardless of your gender, being in an empty home with a stranger exposes you to a significant safety risk. A 2019 National Association of Realtors' report indicated that as many as a third of the agents surveyed had been in a position where they felt unsafe or threatened on the job. The time to think about and to plan for your personal safety is before you are standing alone in a home with a client.

Before you meet with any client, tell a coworker or a family member who you will be with and each address that you plan to visit. If you deviate from your initial itinerary for the day, communicate this with at least one other trustworthy person. Consider downloading a tracking app or an emergency safety app with a panic button on your smartphone.

You also should prepare yourself for a dangerous situation. If you feel threatened, you understandably need to be able to defend yourself. Many real estate agents carry personal protection devices, such as pepper spray, a concealed handgun, or something else. Ensure that you comply with local laws when selecting your protection devices. Taking a personal defense class is also a smart idea.

While you are on a tour showing a client different homes, never let your guard down. Always let the client enter a room in front of you. Carefully position yourself so that there is always a clear path between you and an exit. Some real estate agents may be lulled into feeling a false sense of security because of the reputation of the neighborhood or the fact that the tour is taking place in the daytime. Crimes can occur in all locations and at any hour of the day.

One of the most important safety tips for buyers' real estate agents is to trust your instincts. You may not be able to put your finger on something specific, but something may feel off about a situation. Even if you cannot pinpoint what is wrong, trust your gut.

Prepare for the Unexpected

One of the reasons why you may have been attracted to a career in real estate is because of the variation in your day-to-day routine. The real estate market is consistently changing. At the same time, you are serving the needs of different clients with an ever-changing inventory of homes.

As your experience in your field grows, you will increasingly see the need to anticipate situations before they develop. Your due diligence in serving your clients upfront as well as your expanding knowledge of the industry and your market will help you to be better prepared for each new situation that you face. Look for the educational opportunities that each new experience provides.

12

Commissions

This is a great moment to stop and review how real estate agents actually get paid. That seems important, right?

It's easier if we start at the end of a transaction to better understand things.

So let's say you just represented a seller in the successful sale of their home to a buyer for $500,000. The seller now has to pay the total commission owed on the transaction. Remember, commissions are *always* negotiable and there is no "standard" amount. But for this example, we will say the seller agreed to 4 percent commission total. Assuming the commission is being split equally between the buyer and seller's agent, both agents would receive 2 percent.

Or would they? Well, the brokerage receives the 2 percent, and how much of that the agent gets to take home is determined by your agreement with your employing brokerage. Old-school style, brick-and-mortar type brokerages can charge agents up to 30, 40, even 50 percent or more of the commission from agents, leaving them with just 1 percent in this example. Newer models of real estate brokerages let agents start off on 100 percent commission splits and instead charge a flat fee per transaction. With one of these brokerages, instead of your broker taking 50 percent, they might only take around $600 flat. So in this example we've been using, of the $500,000 home sale at 2 percent commission split paid to both brokerages, that means you'd only take home $5,000 with the old-style broker. But with the newer style, you'd be taking home $9,400. Would you rather have 50 percent or 94 percent? You do the math.

Optimizing your income is understandably an essential priority, and your commission split with your broker plays a significant role in this. However, the commission split that is most advantageous and profitable for you is not always the one that gives you the higher percentage of the split. The reason for this is because of the value of the services and perks offered by the broker.

For example, a broker may take a larger percentage of your commission and offer many high-quality leads in exchange. The end result may be that you earn more money overall than you would if you received no leads or only low-quality leads from the broker.

There are numerous commission-split structures that are used by real estate brokerage firms. You may discover some variations of these common structures as well. What are these structures?

A traditional split is a straight sharing of the commission between the broker and the real estate agent. A variation would yield a higher or lower percentage to the broker based on the support and services provided. It is reasonable to negotiate this split so that it is more favorable to you when you have a consistent record of closing more transactions and when you have established your own lead generation system.

Keep in mind that some of the larger and most well-known brokerage firms also have a separate split on top of the broker's percentage. For example, the top fee may be 5 percent, and the broker's fee may be 50 percent. The remaining 45 percent will go to the real estate agent.

You may find brokers in your area that offer a 100 percent model. Essentially, you keep the entire commission for each transaction. Generally, the broker will charge some type of administrative fee on a monthly basis. The downside to this structure is that you will be responsible for paying the monthly fee even when you do not close any transactions. The upside is that the administrative fee usually remains the same as you become more profitable. Keep in mind that special training and other services may be available for a separate fee as well.

While you may find that 100 percent commission deals have their own hidden costs, tenacious and productive real estate agents make them work. If you're ready to work independently, have a lot of drive, and find the right firm to support you, you'll make huge profits when you take home full commissions.

Some firms also pay their real estate agents a salary. As a result, the real estate agent then becomes an employee. The real estate agent receives regular income, and the employer is responsible for withholding taxes, offering benefits, and more. While this may seem attractive to new real estate agents, there are some potential downsides. For example, your income may be capped by your salary, and the broker will usually have a firm sales quota that you are required to meet. A variation of this would be a lower base salary plus a commission on each closed transaction.

This is a great thing about the real estate industry. There is more than enough business to support all of the different models of operating a real estate brokerage. This competition is great for agents and in turn is also great for consumers. When agents have more flexibility with the commission split being offered to them by their employing brokerage, it gives the agent similar flexibility to reduce or credit their commission to their client in order to help make a deal happen, when necessary. It's win-win.

13

Pricing Strategies and Negotiating Successfully

One of the first questions a potential new client will ask you is, "What is my house worth?" Rest assured that most new clients have already done moderate research. They know what the house down the street sold for, and they often believe that their house is superior to that one in some way. They may also be aware of things like the average increase in housing prices throughout the metropolitan area and other general statistics.

With this in mind, new clients often have a fairly good idea of what they think your answer should be. Often, they are looking for some confirmation that they are on the right track with their own guesstimate.

However, there are many other factors that go into pricing a home than simply knowing what another house nearby sold for. Understanding how to analyze multiple comparables is only one of those factors. For example, you also need to take into account market conditions, the seller's goals, the desired pricing strategy, and more.

You understandably want to earn a new client's business, and you may be aware that the home-owner is talking to other real estate agents as well. However, establishing an appropriate price upfront is one of the most important steps that you can take to ensure that the client's goals are achieved. At the same time, pricing impacts your professional statistics as well as your reputation.

Because of these factors, it is often best to use this stage of your relationship with a new client to establish expectations and to develop rapport. Educating your clients about the reasons behind your numbers and recommendations will help you to position yourself as a market expert. Some sellers want their real estate agent to be a "yes" man, and others are interested in finding a true professional who can help them sell their home soon and for top dollar. Your approach to pricing will set the tone for your relationship and establish expectations going forward.

You can see that pricing a house has far-reaching implications. What does it actually take to price a home competitively and to meet the client's expectations in the process? A closer look at real estate pricing strategies will help you to excel in this critical area.

Comparative Market Analysis

The comparative market analysis is probably the most common pricing analysis method that you will encounter in real estate. Sometimes called a competitive marketing analysis, or a comparable marketing analysis, the CMA is an essential tool in determining market value of a property.

The key to a good comparative market analysis is fresh data, meaning data that is no older than six months. You also want to stay within 10-15 percent of the square footage of the subject property. And any comparable properties shouldn't be any further than half a mile in densely populated areas, or one mile in more sparsely populated areas. You may need to adjust some of these to accommodate the specific conditions in your local market. But once you decide on the variables that you will use to limit the data when begin to pull data from the MLS, you will want to look at sold listings, active listings, and even expired listings.

Sold listings will tell you the average time it takes to sell a property, in terms of days on market. You can also determine the list price to sale price ratio, which tells you whether homes are selling below, at, or above asking price.

Active listings give you an idea of who your competition is. You will want to adjust your price accordingly to make your property stand out from the others.

Finally, expired listings give you a chance to see why other listings did not sell. What do you notice about these expired listings? Are the photos and associated marketing not up to professional standards? Was the pricing out of bounds? The answer to these questions will help you ensure your listing does not end up on the expired list as well.

Taking all of this information together will give you a drilled-down picture of the property's current market value.

You may have heard that a home is worth whatever someone is willing to pay for it. Why does it matter what other homes in the area are selling for if a buyer and seller agree on a price?

For most buyers today, the purchase can only be executed with financing from a home loan. Lenders generally will lend on the lesser of the sales price or the appraised value. This means that the buyer and seller can agree to sell the house for an astronomical amount, but the lender's final loan amount will be based on the appraised value if that amount is lower.

How do appraisers determine the value of a home? They analyze a variety of data points to arrive at a final figure, but they often rely most heavily on comparable market data. Appraisers pull comps from the MLS using the same strategy for selecting properties as you use. Imagine what would happen if the appraised value came in far lower than the sales price weeks down the road. Would the buyer back out? Would the buyer have to come up with a larger down payment because of lending constraints?

Unless you have a cash buyer who is willing to pay an above-market price for the home, recent and local comps will play a role in your initial pricing strategy and in the transaction's final numbers at closing. That being said, there often is some wiggle room with regards to establishing price based on comps. We will dig into that soon.

Selecting the right comps for your transaction is crucial. In addition to choosing nearby properties that have been sold or listed within the last six months, you need to pay attention to how comparable they actually are to your property. Generally, you will choose the three top comps to use. While square footage is important, factors like property condition, amenities, the number of bedrooms and stories, and even curb appeal should also play a role in your selection of the right comps.

No home will be a perfect comparable, so you will need to use your judgment to make pricing adjustments. For example, if you know that the home down the street has recently been renovated and the subject property has not, it is reasonable to make a downward adjustment when using that home as a comp.

Once you have done this for all three of your top comps, you will crunch numbers to arrive at an average price per square foot. Often, a real estate agent will average these three figures together. However, you may find that one of your comps is more closely matched to your subject property, so you may weigh that comp more heavily. Your blended price per square foot will then be applied to the subject property's square footage to reach an estimated value.

This is where the wiggle room comes into play. As you look at other listings in the area, you will see that some homes are priced slightly or well above or below your valuation. Based on basic economic principles, homes that are priced lower may sell more quickly than higher-priced homes when all other relevant factors hold steady.

Depending on the client's price expectations, timing needs, and other factors, a slightly higher or lower list price may be selected. For example, if the seller needs to sell as soon as possible, listing the home slightly below the middle point may be a good strategy.

Seller's and Buyer's Markets

When it comes down to it, real estate is not above the basic economic principles of supply and demand. Knowing this will help you greatly when it comes to determining pricing strategy as well as marketing and negotiating tactics.

In a buyer's market there are more homes listed for sale than there are buyers. This means that, generally speaking, prices are lower, homes are listed on the market for longer, and buyers have more room and power when negotiating with sellers.

A seller's market is the reverse, where there are more buyers than there are listings. This results in homes sitting on the market for less time and homes selling for above asking price. In a seller's market, competition among buyers is fierce, and home sellers can expect an overall easier time negotiating.

The economic principle of supply and demand feeds into everything from how you establish reasonable expectations upfront to your pricing strategy, seller concessions and more. A closer look at buyer's and seller's markets will help you to determine what adjustments you should make to your pricing strategy.

In a buyer's market, there is a general feeling among buyers that a lower-than-asking-price offer will be accepted. The longer a home has been sitting on the market, the stronger this feeling may be. With this in mind, some real estate agents will price a home to move in a buyer's market. They do not want an offer to be discounted simply because of limited buyer activity.

On the other hand, some sellers may be price sensitive. For example, they may not be willing or financially able to accept an offer lower than a certain amount. Perhaps it is commonplace in the market for a seller to pay for some of the closing costs. With this in mind, it may be wise to start the asking price at a slightly higher amount with the knowledge that a buyer will likely start negotiating. With this strategy, your buyer's starting point with negotiations is established higher.

However, when a home is priced too high in a seller's market, there is a chance that no offer will be made. The home may sit on the market for an excessive amount of time, and this can create the impression among buyers that there is something wrong with the home. Because of these factors, price adjustments that you make above or below the supported comp value should be within reason.

In a seller's market, sellers know that their home is in demand, and they want to maximize their return on it. Some sellers may expect a bidding war to break out that drives the price higher. Others may simply want to sell for a reasonable price as soon as possible. Sellers generally may not need to consider below-market offers or entertain unreasonable attempts for negotiations in a seller's market. However, each situation is unique, and all factors will need to be taken into consideration.

Remember that we discussed appraisal comps potentially affecting a buyer's financing. This may be particularly relevant in a seller's market with rapidly increasing housing prices. With this in mind, a list price should be set at a reasonable level based on comps, regardless of market conditions.

If multiple offers are received in a seller's market, one consideration when selecting an offer may be the buyer's prequalification for financing. A prequalification for a lower loan-to-value ratio means that the buyer likely has deeper pockets. As a result, he or she may be in a better financial position to pay an above-market price if the appraisal comes in lower than expected.

Your clients rely on you to keep tabs on market conditions. You must be aware of when a market is showing signs of cooling off or heating up. Often, this will happen while a home is listed on the market.

If this is the case, pricing may need to be adjusted while the listing is active.

Keep in mind that this can impact your comps analysis as well. Market activity can often change dramatically over the course of only a few months. The value on a comp down the street that sold only a few months ago may need to be adjusted because of market changes. With this in mind, you may put more weight on a comp that is a month old and less weight on one that is six months old.

Because market conditions directly and significantly impact many aspects of a real estate transaction, it is your job as a real estate agent to explain current market conditions and their implications to your clients. When you discuss your valuation of the property, market conditions should be a part of the conversation. After all, homes are not sold in a bubble. They are listed in direct competition against others in the marketplace.

Absorption Rate

What is absorption rate—and almost more critical—why is it so important? We'll cover the what, then get to the why. Absorption rate, very simply, is the rate at which homes sell in any area.

And it's actually very easy to figure this out.

First, pick a period of time. Let's just say 12 months. Now what you have to do is figure out the number of homes sold in that area over that period of time.

You can do all homes, you can do condos, single families—it's really up to you. But let's just say, again keeping it simple, that there are only 24 homes sold in this neighborhood. Now what we're going to do is divide the number of homes sold by the number of months, so 24 homes divided by 12 months equals just two homes sold per month.

So what does this mean to us? Well, if four homes are currently for sale. And we know that two homes sell each month. Then four divided by two equals two. These four homes are going to be sold in two months, assuming they're priced appropriately.

Why is this even important? Let's say your client wants to sell their house in just one month, so they can take their dream job in another state. Well, don't you think this would be a good bit of information to know?

Knowing your specific market's absorption rate will tell you a lot about how long your home is going to sit on the market and how much you need to price it to get it sold faster, later, or not at all.

The first 7 to 14 days that a home is listed is when it receives its most attention. So if the property is overpriced, you risk losing out on this essential window for marketing your listing. The longer that a property is listed on the market, the more buyers will view the property negatively and you risk receiving more offers for below asking price. Aside from the negative impact that's improperly priced homes have for the seller, there are also negative impacts to your business. Your list-to-sell ratio will be negatively impacted when the property sells for below the list price. You will upset your sellers and risk the chance for repeat and referral business. And your competition will use it to show that they are better marketers and more deserving of the next listing opportunity.

It can sometimes seem easier to just agree to mist the home for whatever the sellers are asking for so that you can get the listing, but you will soon regret that for the above reasons. In reality, it is actually easier in the short term and the long term to educate your sellers on the appropriate pricing strategy, and if the sellers are unwilling to listen to your advice, consider declining the listing if their expectations are too far removed from reality. You will save yourself weeks of heartache and stress. Plus, when their overpriced listing inevitably expires, you can attempt to swoop in and pick up the listing, ideally without gloating about how you were right—even though the temptation to do so will be strong.

Putting It All Together

Now that you have a better understanding of the many factors that drive list prices, it is important to pull your knowledge together. How does this relate to your next client meeting?

Because so many aspects of valuation are based on the home itself, including its style, condition, layout, and more, you cannot realistically create a valuation on a home without touring it. With this in mind, you should schedule an initial meeting with a new client to tour the home. This is a quick walk-through where you spend a few minutes walking around the interior and exterior of the home. You will get an idea of its features, finishes, and all-around appeal.

During this initial meeting, spend a few minutes speaking with the homeowner about his or her hot buttons. Does the homeowner need to sell quickly because a job offer is taking him out of town? Is she willing to wait a little longer to receive a higher offer? Use this time to identify a rough payoff amount for the existing mortgage, future plans to relocate, and any other factors that may be relevant to the client.

While comps and market conditions will dictate price and timing when selling a home, the seller understandably has a host of additional factors to consider. Your job is to facilitate a suitable transaction for the seller. Many sellers allow emotions to play a role in their expectations for price and timing. The initial meeting is a time to assess expectations and to explain what your next steps are. This is when you bring up the subject of market comps and sales data, but you will not dig too deeply into the numbers at this stage in the process.

Before leaving the initial meeting, make plans to return a few days later to discuss your findings. This is when you will present your CMA report and openly discuss pricing with the client.

Your second meeting with your client will be much more in-depth, and it will be focused on your CMA report. Ideally, you will provide a copy of the report to each party present. This enables them to follow along with your valuation analysis step by step.

Remember that some sellers may have never seen a CMA report before, and others may have limited experience with them. Because of this, each page of the report should be reviewed in detail. Explain how you selected your comps, what valuation adjustments were made, and why. After the comps, talk about other relevant factors, such as market conditions and the absorption rate.

Your clients ultimately should have the final say when determining how much they list their home for. As a general rule of thumb, however, you should offer three options. These are a middle option that is perfectly aligned with market comps, a higher price that likely will yield a longer time on the market, and a lower price that may potentially leave money on the table.

From a professional perspective, it is important to ask yourself if you can realistically sell the house for the homeowner's preferred price and in a reasonable period of time. Unrealistic expectations inevitably lead to unhappy clients, poor reviews, and bad word-of-mouth advertising. This can cause significant harm to your reputation and your business as a whole. You can and should be frank with a potential client if you have concerns.

While pricing strategies are rooted in analytics and require ample number crunching, you can see that there are soft components to developing a suitable strategy as well. You now have deeper knowledge to help you create winning strategies today, and you may refine your approach through hands-on experience over the years.

Negotiating Successfully

The art of negotiation includes two or more parties attempting to find a common middle ground that is beneficial to both sides. Real estate negotiations usually end up with one or more parties compromising, or settling on mutually agreeable points. A sales transaction can literally have hundreds of potential variables. To best serve the negotiation process, a purchase contract offer can be adapted in many different ways. Details such as the price, closing time range, seller credits, and the requested loan contingency time periods for numerous contractual checklist items (e.g., loan qualification, home inspection report, appraisal) can all be modified.

Remember: The real estate sales process goes smoothest when each side of the negotiation table walks away feeling as if they have won something important to them.

Be Proactive, Not Reactive

During real estate negotiations, it's better to be proactive rather than reactive. It's important to stay positive, act from a position of strength, communicate clearly, and listen with empathy. Try to avoid being negative and reactive, acting from a position of weakness, and not listening to the other party's true needs and interests.

"We have two ears and one mouth so that we can listen twice as much as we speak." – Epictetus

Sadly, most people prefer to speak more than listen during hotly contested real estate negotiations. This often leads to no deal for anyone (a "lose-lose" situation). Listen closely to the other party. They are likely telling you the easiest way to find the quickest solutions.

More Questions = More Positive Results

In order to close a deal, both parties need to be flexible and open-minded. Be willing to compromise and change your own mind. When trying to persuade someone else to change their mind, get them to focus on questioning their own perceptions or statements.

In debates, many people will focus on a definitive statement made by the other party, such as "you're wrong" or "the roof is one hundred percent fine with no leaks," as opposed to questioning their own beliefs. Changing one's mind first begins with changing the way we ask ourselves the most empowering questions. Questioning our own thoughts, in turn, leads to a more flexible and open mindset.

For example, one party may say emphatically, "I will walk away from this negotiation table if you don't agree to give me a ten thousand dollar credit to fix the roof leaks." A more positive way to express this same concern is to ask the seller questions like, "How much do you think a professional roofer will charge to fix the water leaks?" or "What sort of sales price reduction or credit can you offer us in exchange for this roof situation?" This way, the other party feels that they are the ones offering mutually beneficial solutions.

To increase your odds of success, use the following key strategies when conducting real estate negotiations.

- Have a positive attitude. Smile, be positive, and make the other side feel welcome and appreciated. At the true core, we all just wanted to be liked or loved. Be likable, and the other side will want to make you happy.
- Negotiate in person, instead of online or by phone. We react more to other people's voice tones and body language, both consciously and subconsciously, than to their spoken words. When using email or texts to negotiate, tones and intentions are not easily understood. Someone may be offended by a typed comment that was truly benign, neutral, or even meant to be funny.
- Check your body language. Don't sit in the conference room with your arms and legs crossed. This conveys to other people that you may be closed-minded, angry (another side of fear), reactive, or hard to please. A better option is to have open posture and a smile on your face. Try to look the other people in the eye as much as possible to help you seem more honest and trustworthy. Same applies even if you are on the phone. Did you know

that smiling while speaking makes your voice sound friendlier and warmer? This is due to the way the vocal chords are stretched as we smile. So even though the person on the other end of line can't *see* your smile, they can certainly *hear* it!

- Find common ground. Create a list of items that both sides can agree on toward the start of the meeting. Then, focus on resolving the other issues that need to be worked out with some form of compromise. If the other side doesn't agree with the options you present, provide them with alternative options backed with solid evidence.
- Do not become emotionally attached to the deal. Even if you desperately need the commission for this one real estate deal, please don't act out of reactive fear. Ironically, the fear of losing the deal can be sensed by others in the room and, in turn, can push them away. Deal with the facts of the real estate transaction as opposed to the emotions.
- Show your good sense of humor, when appropriate. Once another person smiles or laughs, they will become more open-minded and receptive.
- End the negotiations on a good note. Before walking out of the room, make sure everyone feels positive about the outcome of the real estate negotiations that have just taken place. Shake hands, thank each side for their participation, and talk about the next positive steps in the process.

Few things in real estate will make you smile more than a satisfying and productive negotiation outcome. If the other side is smiling too, then that is the sign of a very healthy and profitable sales transaction. It means you are well on your way to mastering the art of real estate negotiations.

14

How to Improve Your Sales Skills

Every real estate agent should always be looking for ways to improve their sales skills. Whether you are new to the industry or are simply looking to boost your sales and climb the ladder, there are always strategies for improving your sales skills that could have a significant impact and allow you to enhance your reputation. It can take time and effort to develop these skills but, ultimately, this is what you need to do to get ahead in this industry, which can be highly competitive and hard to stand out from the crowd.

Improve Your Interpersonal Skills

One of the most effective strategies is to improve your interpersonal skills, as this will make a huge difference in your ability to connect with people. While it is true that some people are naturally better at communicating than others, it is possible to develop interpersonal skills, but it can require stepping out of your comfort zone. There are lots of helpful resources online, and it is then a matter of practicing what you learn in real-life situations.

Listen to Your Clients

A successful real estate client understands the value of listening to the client instead of showing them a property and telling them what they need. Listening is an incredibly powerful tool that allows you to get a greater understanding of your client's wants and needs while allowing you to form an important bond with them.

Be Honest

Real estate agents get a bad rep, and this means that people are often skeptical and hesitant when shown around a property. It is for this reason why honesty is so important if you want to make a good impression and sell a property. Never lie, and if you do not know the answer to one of their questions, then admit this and tell them that you will find out as soon as possible; people will appreciate the honesty, and it will help you to stand out from stereotypical real estate agents.

Do Your Research

Ideally, you will always know the answer to a client's questions because you will have done your research. Hard work is key to success in the real estate game, and knowing each property like your own home will help you to portray it in the best light. Make sure to answer any questions and show your client why this is a property that suits their wants and needs. You must also know the market so that you can quickly identify the right properties to show your clients and get there before the competition.

Stay Current on Industry Trends

Similarly, you need to be aware of news and trends that are currently affecting the real estate industry and be able to stay with the times. This can be achieved by reading blogs, signing up to newsletters, joining online communities, and following key figures on social media.

Find a Mentor

Much like in any industry, it can be helpful to have a mentor who can provide you with advice, guidance, and support throughout your career. Real estate agents often make the same mistakes and fall into the same bad habits when first starting out, but if you have an experienced agent in your corner, it can help you to avoid these mistakes and make the right career choices.

Build a Network

Leading on from this, it is also important that you build a large network over the course of your career; this be helpful for a number of reasons. It is helpful to have strong professional relationships with other real estate agents, buyers and sellers, home inspectors, mortgage loan officers, and other key figures in the industry. Networking online is one effective way to build up your contact list, but keep in mind that meeting people face-to-face is much more memorable, so look to attend any industry events and do not shy away from introducing yourself.

Be Professional and Presentable

You need to make a great first impression on your clients because otherwise they will go into viewing with a negative mindset. This means that you should always be friendly yet professional and never late. Additionally, you should always look presentable and look after yourself to make a good first impression.

Be Easy to Contact

You do not want to miss out on a sale because you did not pick up the phone or reply to an email in time. This means that you need to be easy to contact, so keep your phone on you at all times, stay on top of your emails throughout the week, and keep in mind that many people prefer to send a text message in today's day and age, so encourage clients to do this.

Follow Up with Every Lead

Following on from this, you should also follow up every lead so that nothing ever slips through the cracks. Keep all lead details in one place (like your smartphone) including details such as their budget, timeframe, and what properties they are interested in and then be sure to keep checking in with them.

Embrace New Technology

Technology is constantly improving and transforming industries, including the real estate industry. Staying current with this technology and embracing it will be key to success now and in the future and could help you to stay ahead of the curve.

Seek Feedback

It can be hard, but the best way to improve is to seek feedback so that you can identify what your strengths and weaknesses are. It can be hard to give yourself an honest critique, and there may be bad habits that you have picked up that you are unaware of. Seeking feedback from others can help you to turn weaknesses into strengths to become a more complete and successful real estate agent.

Working on your sales skills is crucial for success in the real estate industry, whether you are new to the game or if you are simply looking to improve your conversion rates. The above are all highly effective strategies which should help you to sell more properties and improve your reputation as an agent.

15

Achieve Open House Success

Whether you're a seasoned real estate agent or you're new to the industry, you can always improve your open house game. Aside from the obvious benefit from hosting open houses of getting the home sold faster, agents also stand to impress future home sellers, and today's looky-loos are tomorrows buyers needing an agent, so the savviest open house hosts diligently collect contact information of visitors and then relentlessly stay in touch so when the time is right, the choice for their agent is obvious. To help you step up your open house game, consider these steps the pros take.

Talk to Neighbors

One of the best markets to tap into when it comes to selling real estate is the people who live in your listing's community.

Why?

First, many people who have lived in the community for a long time probably like their area and have attachments to schools, work, etc. For that reason, they may be wanting to stick around but may also be eyeing an upgrade that could pique their interest in the property you're representing.

Second, a lot of people who love their community have friends and family members who want to move in. Because of that, if you advertise your listing to neighbors, those neighbors may advertise your listing to their personal networks.

When engaging neighbors for an open house, we recommend knocking on doors and inviting people personally to a "neighborhood-only" open house event. This event can take place the evening before your mass-market open house.

Not only can this event serve as an excellent test run for you to work out open house kinks, but it can also serve as an awesome way to network with people who may want you to represent their homes in the future.

Ditch the Alcohol

Offering free alcohol at open houses may seem like a good idea, but truth be told, it provides little in the way of value to your event.

Unless you're dealing with high-rollers who expect to be treated to a high-end experience, all alcohol will do is drive up your event's budget and possibly make you liable for your guest's actions if they get too intoxicated.

Remember, it's better to have 10 people walk through your open house who are genuinely interested in your listing than 100 people who just stop by for free drinks.

Live Stream Your Open House

Not everyone who is interested in your open house will be able to attend. To help people attend your open house without actually being there, we love any open house ideas that involve live streaming the event.

Live streams can take place on Periscope, Facebook, or your website.

Costs involved with live streaming can be zero since all you need to live stream through social media platforms is an account and a mobile phone, making this a free and effective way to extend your event's reach.

Don't Forget Low-Tech Touches

Yes, live stream your event, promote it to your email list, post about it on Instagram. But don't neglect low-tech touches.

While every real estate book and blog you read about open house ideas is going to tout the power of the internet (this one included), few take the time to remind you that putting up those five dollar "OPEN HOUSE" signs on the corners of streets can do wonders for foot traffic.

So get those signs set up. Put door hangers around the community.

Low-fi touches like that can seriously boost your event's attendance.

Offer Multiple Digital Staging Renderings

One of the top reasons why people pass on making offers on houses is because they can't see the potential of a space. The best way to allow them to see what you see is to render your vision in reality.

To do that, have multiple digital renderings of different furniture layouts set on an easel in each room of your home. Also, include those digital renderings in a follow-up email or on printouts you offer at your event.

By providing renderings to clients, you'll increase your number of interested buyers big-time.

Don't Forget the Essentials

Real estate agents can get so caught up in clever open house marketing ideas that they forget to provide prospects with the essentials.

For us, essentials include a packet that contains a home's floor plan, renderings of digital stagings, information about the HOA (if applicable), a list of frequently asked questions, your asking price, and contact information.

Armed with that packet, your prospects will be able to make an informed decision on whether or not to engage further.

Time Your Open House Strategically

Everyone does the 1-3 p.m. weekend open house. To counteract, try 4-6 p.m. or 3-5 p.m. The benefit here is that there is less competition, meaning buyers won't have to choose between touring your listing or another one at the same time. Plus, anything that sets you apart from the competition is generally a good thing.

During the week, schedule your open houses keeping in mind that most people are at work. Try for a 6:30 - 8 p.m. event and offer snacks.

You'll find that a lot of professional, qualified buyers will appreciate you working with their schedule.

From timing your event correctly to valuing your listing's neighbors, there is no shortage of small details you can tackle to boost the success of your open house dramatically.

Real estate listings can be the lifeblood of a lucrative career. However, everything from the clients you choose to work with to your marketing expertise, your pricing strategies, and your skills with listing presentations will dictate how successful you will be as a seller's agent. With this in mind, these are key areas to focus on for professional development going forward.

16

It's Never Too Early to Plan for Retirement

Successful real estate agents spend a large portion of their professional lives building up their businesses. They strategically create plans for capturing leads, nurturing leads, building relationships, and more. However, planning for the end of their career often falls to the wayside. If you fail to define what your end game is and outline how you plan to get there, you may never reach your goal.

When real estate commissions roll in on a fairly regular basis, the thought of exiting the business may rarely or never cross your mind. You are, after all, busy serving your clients and growing your business. However, there will come a day when most real estate agents either need or want to hang up their hat and move on to the next chapter in life.

If your next real estate commission were your last one, would you be financially prepared to support yourself fully for the next several decades until the end of your life? If you are like many other real estate agents, there is a quick, clear answer to this question. No.

When to Start Preparing for Retirement

It is never too soon to start planning and saving for your non-working years, but how can you get started? There are three primary strategies for retirement planning. One strategy is to live off a lump sum of capital and to progressively chip away on that capital over time. Another strategy is to develop income streams and live off those income streams for the rest of your life. The final option is to blend these strategies together. As you might imagine, it can take time to develop these strategies in the best of circumstances.

For W-2 workers, the typical retirement plan revolves around depositing equal sums of cash into a 401(k) or an IRA. This works well for these workers because they receive steady income throughout the year, but you need to take a different approach. Because you are a real estate agent whose sole or primary source of income is based on commissions, you may not be able to make equal monthly deposits into an IRA or 401(k) account. Instead, you may be able to allocate lump sums of cash into your account irregularly and based on when deals close.

With careful planning and concerted effort, you may be able to eventually save enough money in a traditional retirement account to retire. However, you may not have the luxury of predetermining a retirement date. After all, you cannot know with certainty how much money you will earn next year or even next month. Because of this, you cannot know how much money you will be able to allocate toward retirement. Regardless of what your retirement plan is, it is clear that you need to set the wheels in motion today. Doing so gives you the best opportunity for achieving your goals.

Your Estimated Financial Need in Retirement

If you Google "how much money you need to save in retirement," you will likely see an estimate of between 60 to 80 percent of your current, pretaxed income. Is this realistic for you? While you can use this rough estimate to begin planning, a better approach involves digging into each line item in your budget. Retirement looks different for everyone. Because of this, it makes sense to prepare a detailed budget rather than to use rough, one-size-fits-all estimations.

For example, if your current mortgage payment is $2,000, will that realistically drop to $1,200, or 60 percent, in retirement? This could happen for some people, but the reality is that your future housing payment could look drastically different based on what you plan to do in retirement. After all, living on an expensive yacht and touring coastlines around the world comes with a boat loan payment, boat insurance, mooring fees, and more.

To create a post-retirement budget, look at the expenses that you plan to still have in retirement.

These may include bills for your smartphone, food, car payment, auto insurance, and more. Will these expenses drop by 60 to 80 percent in retirement? In all likelihood, your recurring expenses like these will be significantly higher many years from now at the start of your retirement because of inflation. More than that, they may continue to increase dramatically throughout your retirement. Your retirement plan should take into account the likelihood of escalating expenses.

You may plan to own your car free and clear when you retire, but you likely will need to replace that car at least once or twice in retirement. Will you take a lump sum of cash out of your retirement capital to replace the car as needed, or will you increase your monthly budget by taking out a car loan? Your plan of action for this expense can play a major role in your overall retirement needs.

After you look at these and other expenses that you plan to still have after retirement, look at new expenses. For example, you may not have a house payment, but you may have an RV payment instead. This may come with costs for RV insurance, maintenance, fuel, and a nightly fee for a pad or camping site. Unless you plan to stay in the house that you own throughout your retirement, you will need to dig deep by researching all of the related costs for your preferred alternatives. Remember to adjust the costs for inflation as you plan ahead.

Finally, think about how you plan to spend your days in retirement. You should have a healthy allocation of funds for everything from your golf club membership to bingo, day trips, and more. After all, most people do not plan to sit in the house in front of the television every day of their retirement.

You can see that using a rough estimate like 60 to 80 percent of current expenses to create a retirement budget likely will not get you to a realistic figure. After you have created a working budget for these expenses, remember to factor in things like prescription drugs, medical care, a contingency fee for unexpected expenses, holiday spending, and more.

After you have created a line-item budget that estimates all of your monthly retirement expenses, you have a good idea of how much money you need in order to live your picture-perfect retirement. Now, you are ready to answer the next important question: After you retire from real estate and the commission checks stop rolling in, how will you cover all of those expenses on a monthly basis?

How to Pay for Retirement

As mentioned earlier, there are three primary ways to pay for your expenses in retirement. One of these is to pull money out of your established accounts. An example of this would be distributions from a retirement account. With this method, the capital would eventually be depleted. The second method is to establish income streams that do not deplete capital. For example, income-producing real estate investments may continue to produce a profit for decades, and their value may increase rather than decrease over time. The third method is to create a healthy balance between the two options. A closer look at these methods is in order before you choose the method that is best for you.

There are a variety of tax-advantaged retirement plans that are popular with self-employed workers. All of the tax-advantaged plans have an annual cap on contribution amounts. While account growth will depend on the investments that you select, the growth will be capped to some extent by the contribution limit. Because of the annual contribution cap on all tax-advantaged retirement plans, you should plan to spend many years contributing to your accounts before retiring.

In addition, be aware you will be penalized for early withdrawals from these accounts. Do you plan to work until you are of retirement age, or would you like to plan for an early retirement? If the latter is aligned with your goals, how will you pay your monthly expenses until you can take retirement account distributions? Your retirement plan must include some way to cover your expenses for this period of time.

Because of the tax advantages of IRAs, 401(k) accounts, and others, it makes sense for many real estate agents to utilize them fully. However, distributions may not be sufficient to fully fund all of your retirement plans. Social Security income continues to be enjoyed, but there have been questions about its reliability as a future income source for decades. To err on the side of caution, it may be best to assume that this income will not be available to you.

There are a few options available for rounding out your retirement plan. For example, you could take on a part-time job or start a money-making hobby after you move on to the next chapter in your life. While some people enjoy working in a low-stress job after retirement, others would prefer to simply never work again.

With this in mind, what are some realistic ways that you can make money in retirement throughout the rest of your life? Some of the more common sources of retirement income are rental properties, dividends, royalties, business income, and a CD ladder. A closer look at the various types of retirement accounts and income-producing assets in the next sections will help you to create a better plan for your retirement.

Take Stock of Your Current Situation

Now that you have a better idea of what it takes to retire comfortably and what it will take to get yourself to that point, you are ready to act. This process begins when you take stock of your current situation, and it continues when you define what you expect from your retirement.

After you crunch all of the numbers and begin planning, you may be one of many people who discover that you cannot bridge the gap between your current status and your desired retirement. There are a few strategies that you can take if that is the case. For example, you could adjust your lifestyle so that you can afford to save and invest more money now.

On the other hand, you could scale back your retirement plans so that you need less money down the road. You could also readjust your allocation of income-producing assets. This may require you to divert some assets away from low-risk investments. If you choose to make this move, do so only after you have carefully reviewed all of your options and are comfortable with the potential outcomes.

Remember to revisit your retirement plan frequently. At the same time, monitor the progress of your efforts. By taking these steps, you can ensure that you stay on track and can retire at or close to your target date.

17

Your Future in Real Estate

Are you waiting to sit for your licensing exam? Perhaps you are searching for a broker to sponsor you, or maybe you simply do not know how to gain traction now that all of the basics are in place. The reality is that new real estate agents must find their own way through the fog, and every real estate agent who has come before you has stood in your shoes.

There is comfort in knowing that you are not alone, but intimidation can set in as well. Unfortunately, by now, the majority of those individuals who have stood in your shoes have given up on their dream of being successful real estate agents. They have moved on to a new chapter in their lives. Thankfully, that outcome does not need to be your future.

Through this guide, your eyes have been opened about everything from establishing client relationships to using proven pricing strategies, refining marketing techniques, improving sales skills, and more.

You have also undoubtedly learned just how much you still have to learn. Where can you go from here?

The Next Steps

As a successful real estate agent, it is important to continue looking for new growth opportunities. This may include opportunities to learn more about your market, to gain insight on a new marketing technique, or to take a bona fide continuing-education class for professional credit. In fact, professional growth and improvement are so important that you should consider incorporating this aspect of your job into your weekly or monthly schedule. After all, if you do not make time for personal growth, it is less likely to happen.

At the same time, networking is essential for professional success as a real estate agent. By now, you may have heard a hundred times that real estate is a relationship business. Without a focus on building and nurturing relationships, you may have a hard time achieving your vision of what a successful real estate career looks like. With this in mind, always look for ways to meet new people. Refine your people skills so that you know how to turn an initial introduction into a lead and how to turn a lead into a client. Even those with extensive people skills may have room to improve in this area. As is the case with education, structure networking and relationship building into your weekly or monthly schedule as a unique section so that they become priorities.

It can take years of hard work to build up momentum in this field even with the best plan in place. It is easy to lose focus or to give up on yourself. Perseverance is just as important as education and networking. With this in mind, it is important to create a safety net. Who can you turn to when you are starting to feel frustrated? As a new real estate agent, the only person who may come to mind right now is your broker. That is understandable. As you expand your professional network, be aware that not all valuable relationships lead to sales. Focus on developing a few relationships centered around support.

Your Real Estate Business

If you do not already have a business plan, now is the right time to create one. You may work under a broker, but you are an independent contractor with your own business to grow. Often, new real estate agents view the end goal of getting licensed as closing deals. There are no future plans or specific goals beyond closing deals.

Ask yourself a few questions. Do you plan to break into a specific territory? Do you intend to specialize in a niche? Do you eventually want to create a team or become a broker? While you obviously want to close more deals, what else do you want to accomplish in your career?

Closing deals is your short-game plan. You need to refine your marketing plan, build relationships, and more in order to close deals and achieve your financial goals. Those deals should also be stepping stones for your long-game plan. When you think beyond the next commission check, you can properly steer your career for growth.

Your business plan may include a one-year plan for closing your first few deals. It may also cover important matters like developing a website, building leads, and growing relationships. When you think beyond that first year to your third or fifth year in the business, you are forced to think about what it takes to get from here to there. You can then incorporate those important stepping stones into your one-year plan. By doing so, you have a legitimate plan for doing more than just closing deals. You have a plan for success as a real estate agent.

A Final Word

When you started reading this guide, you understandably held high hopes for your career as a real estate agent. You were eager to get the ball rolling, but you did not know how to start. Perhaps you thought you had a good idea of where to go, but you wanted guidance on getting from point A to point B. Now, you may realize that you need to reimagine what your career as a real estate agent will look like and how you will manage professional growth and development.

This guide provides you with an excellent foundation that you can build on. Consider referring back to it in the months and years ahead to ensure that you remain focused on the core principles.

Remember that there is always more to learn. There is always room to grow. By embracing those principles early in your career, you can be in a better position for success as you take your next steps.

Printed in Great Britain
by Amazon